# Invitation

# to a War

## My Early War Experience at
## Pearl Harbor and Guadalcanal

## Larry A. Drew

These personal memoirs have been published
in loving memory of our father, Larry A. Drew, in
recognition of the 75th Anniversary of the Attack of
Pearl Harbor

May we always remember.

Cover:  *USS Arizona.* The forward superstructure and Number Two
14/45 triple gun turret afire after the Japanese raid, 7 December 1941.
The foremast is leaning as a result of the collapse of the hull structure
below its front leg, following the explosion of the ship's forward
magazines.  US Navy Photo NH 97379

ISBN-10: 0-9981927-0-8

ISBN-13: 978-0-9981927-0-3

In honor of the courageous and determined men
with whom I worked and fought at Pearl Harbor
and Guadalcanal

# About the Author

Larry A. Drew was born in 1921 in Tappen, North Dakota, and spent his early years on the family ranch. The Great Depression forced a move to Bismarck, North Dakota, before resettling to his grandmother's farm in Westboro, Ohio.

Larry attended Jefferson High School in Westboro, where he proved a very able student, and "got the notion" to go to college. This was a first for the family, and his ambition was not met with parental enthusiasm! He spent two years at Ohio State University, where his subjects included ROTC. In 1941 he took a job with Allis-Chalmers in Cincinnati, to earn and save money to finish his degree. Larry eventually achieved his dream, earning his Bachelors degree at the University of California, Berkeley, but not until 1948. In between were several years when "all hell broke loose!"

This book tells the story of the first half of those incredibly difficult and perilous war years, at Pearl Harbor and Guadalcanal. Larry returned from the Pacific to the U.S. to attend Officer Candidate School. There he was recruited for "hazardous duty" and found himself serving with the OSS in Burma and China until the end of the war, the subject of another book.

After the war Larry married, began a family, and was invited to help build a new organization, the CIA, based on his OSS experiences. A few years later, the Pacific Coast beckoned, and he found himself again working at a US Naval Shipyard, this one at Long Beach, California, as Financial Manager. After retiring from government service in the 1980s, he worked as construction manager for Disneyland's remodel of Fantasyland. He passed away peacefully in his sleep on September 2, 2000, exactly 55 years after the signing of the Surrender of Japan. He now rests with his brothers in arms at the Black Hills National Cemetery in South Dakota.

# CONTENTS

## Chapter 1. Hawaii Bound

## Chapter 2. First Week at the Shipyard

# Chapter 3.
# December 7th & Aftermath – War

# Chapter 4.
# Goodbye Navy, Hello Army – May 31, 1942

## Chapter 4.  (Continued)
## Goodbye Navy, Hello Army – May 31, 1942

## Chapter 5.
## On Board the *Noordam* – Destination Unknown
## November 25, 1942

# Chapter 6.
# Guadalcanal – December 1942

## Chapter 6.  (Continued)
## Guadalcanal – December 1942

## Chapter 7.  New Caledonia

## Chapter 8.  Homeward Bound

# Chapter 1.
# Hawaii Bound

## Pearl Harbor Labor Board:
## An Invitation to Travel

During the summer of 1941, I was working on the graveyard shift at Allis Chalmers in Cincinnati, and attending the University of Cincinnati during the day. Allis Chalmers had converted from heavy industry to defense work, and I was an inspector on my shift.

Four or five of the young machinists became friendly, and we would visit on occasion as I was checking their machined lathe work for accuracy. They had heard that the Navy Shipyard at Pearl Harbor had begun looking Stateside for new employees to augment the staff of shipyard workers at Pearl Harbor. Each of us wrote the Pearl Harbor employment office and requested application papers.

When my application papers arrived, I didn't bother to fill them out, nor did I return any papers to Pearl Harbor. A few weeks later, however, I received in the mail a medical form that I was to take to a physician, who would give me a physical exam, fill out the medical form, and return it to the Pearl Harbor Labor Board. I didn't bother with these papers either; nor did I communicate anything back to the Labor Board.

A few weeks later, I received an unexpected invitation in the mail, in the form of a Request for Transportation from the Pearl Harbor Labor Board. This, when presented at the railroad ticket office in Cincinnati, would be exchanged for one first-class railroad ticket with Pullman lower berth for myself from Cincinnati, Ohio to Vallejo, California. It also provided an advance of funds for travel expenses and instructions to report to the Labor Board at Mare Island Navy Yard, Vallejo, California for ocean transportation on to Pearl Harbor!

On this set of papers I acted and followed through. I visited Dad at Westboro and bade him goodbye, packed my suitcase, boarded the train, and set off across country. The changing farm-scape scenery was interesting through Indiana, Illinois, and Missouri. Then came the plains-state scenery of Oklahoma, and the desert states, and into Reno, Nevada – a small western town of perhaps 10,000 persons stretching along the railroad track. From Reno, we climbed into the Sierra Nevada Mountains – passing through the snowsheds which kept the tracks clear of snowslides – down the other side of the mountains, through the Great Central Valley of California, and finally on into Vallejo on the northeastern shore of San Pablo Bay.

It was late afternoon when I reached the Mare Island Navy Yard. I was told at the Labor Board to put up at the local hotel for the night and return at 08:00 next morning back at the Labor Board.

I was back next morning, as told. Processing was swift at the Labor Board: a matter of assuring that you had arrived for water transportation and then being taken down to pierside and boarded on a Navy transport. In my case, it was the *USS Henderson* – a World War I vessel, still in service in 1941. Already aboard was the entire troop complement of the Fourth Defense Battalion, U.S. Marine Corps. They were waiting for the fifteen or so civilians headed for Pearl Harbor before the ship could depart.

Figure 1. *USS Henderson* circa 1933. US Navy Photo NH 99308

# Aboard the *USS Henderson*

We civilians were escorted to quarters by a Navy chief petty officer and briefed on what was expected of us while on board. We each had a troopship bunk identical to those given the Marines. Bunks were in stacks, six high: long enough to lie down, slightly wider than one's shoulders, and a comfort zone of about twelve inches between one's face and the bottom-side of the bunk above.

In all things, the Marines came first: first to shower, first to eat, first to use any and all deck space, etc. As civilians, we would stand at the end of their chow line and eat at the same mess, with the same military hardware, and served the same food. When they had cleared the showers, we were free to make use of them and warned to expect no luxury. All plumbing was hooked to salt water: showers, toilets, lavatories, etc. Soap didn't lather with salt water and left one feeling sticky afterward, but we were assured that we were just as clean as if fresh water had been available.

The chief petty officer was our assigned shepherd while we were on board. He herded us out of the way of the Marines, saw

3

to it that we kept our grumbling down and our disturbances to a minimum. One quickly got the idea that civilians were something less than first-class passengers – as far as the rest of the ship was concerned.

All that day and night, the coast of California slid by on our left as we headed south. Early next morning, the ship put into port and tied up at the Navy pier in San Pedro. There, the day was spent taking on fuel, fresh water, provisions, and mail for Hawaiian military bases. Next day, early, *Henderson* put to sea again, and soon the California coastline and mountains became lost in the distance behind.

*Henderson* was a slow ship, said by the Navy to be capable of eleven knots per hour with a following sea and the movie sail up! At this speed, we were placing about 300 miles behind us each day, and Hawaii was some 2,000-plus miles ahead! *Henderson* took a course far to the south, avoiding all shipping lanes. Only one ship was seen en route. It was hailed, didn't reply; hailed again and no reply. *Henderson* placed a shot across her bow, and this time the hailed ship replied most promptly! Identification, port of departure, registry, destination, cargo, etc. were quickly manifest, and she was finally given permission to proceed. All this in open ocean, far from land anywhere. No other vessels were seen between San Pedro and Honolulu.

During the days on shipboard, I met and became friends with a young Marine, Andy Armstrong. Much of our free time was spent together. I learned much personally about Andy and about my surroundings. Andy liked the Marine Corps; boot camp training had been really tough, and he had three more years to serve of a four-year enlistment. The Fourth Defense Battalion was equipped and trained for the defense of United States Pacific island possessions, and, as such, was armed with large-caliber, shore-defense, long-range guns and large, fast-firing, anti-aircraft guns. The troops were to remain on board

*Henderson* at Pearl Harbor while she took on fuel and supplies; then *Henderson* would depart and deliver the battalion at Midway Island, where it would remain for the next two years. Addresses were exchanged, and Andy would write to me after he became established.

Navy chow was quite good, as well as plentiful. The only stipulation given us was that the food accepted on one's mess tray all had to be consumed – none discarded. To assure this, a mess petty officer stood at the place where mess trays were turned in for scullery, just to make certain that there were no finicky eaters on board. Both Navy and Marine Corp personnel seemed to resent the handful of civilians onboard. The reason: we were scheduled for jobs at the Pearl Harbor Navy Yard with big wages, plentiful overtime, and freedom to do as we wished with our spare time.

The materiel of the battalion was on board another ship and would be delivered offshore at Midway, coinciding with the arrival of the *Henderson*. This cargo included all of the guns, ammunition, fuel, generators, fresh water, food, field kitchens, tents, and all else required to support a lengthy stay of 1,000 Marines on a sandy, treeless island located over a thousand miles from any resupply or support base of any kind.

Figure 2. Diamond Head.
US Army photo reprinted from *The 25th Division and World War 2* (p 12), Cpt. Robert F. Karolevitz, ed., 1946, Army and Navy Publishing Co.

# Pearl Harbor in Sight:
# First Impressions

And then one morning, a bosun on deck let out a shout. "There it is!" he roared. "Way over there – Diamond Head! We're coming in!" Men on his side of the ship looked and strained for a view, and eventually each could see a dark shadow resembling the tip of a rose thorn, definitely solid and unmoving – far off on the horizon. As *Henderson* continued to thump along at the same dogged speed, the thorn tip continued to grow in size and shape. Another couple of hours gave it the stature of a good-sized hill, followed after time by the outline of a city along the shore: Honolulu and the Aloha Tower at the edge of the city harbor.

On past the city and harbor, the *Henderson* thumped along. We passed the large hangars of the Army Air Base at Hickam

Field, and then we could see the towering "hammerhead crane" at the Navy Yard. Soon, *Henderson* executed a right turn and entered an obvious opening into a wide channel – passing small Navy craft, buoys, and work craft. Big ships began appearing such as I had never seen before. I learned that some were minelayers and minesweepers, others destroyers; still larger ships were the battle cruisers, and the obvious giants: the battleships. There was a time when I could recite the names of all. Now, my memory has dimmed, but I still recall many of the battleships: *Arizona, Pennsylvania, West Virginia, California, Oklahoma, Nevada, Utah*, and *Tennessee*. The huge battle cruisers: *Helena, Honolulu, Baltimore, Raleigh*, and *St. Louis*...and now my memory fades.

The "hammerhead crane" was so named because of its appearance being similar to an upended hammer. Dry Dock Number 1, a sight to see, was 1,000 feet long and located almost under the towering crane. It held two destroyers, the *Cassin* and the *Downes*, located side by side at the forward end. The battleship *Pennsylvania* was directly behind in the same dock. The dry dock was enormous, large enough to accommodate the largest aircraft carrier of the fleet. Directly outboard of Dry Dock No. 1 was a new and even larger dry dock, complete but for the placing of reinforcing steel and the pouring of a massive concrete floor.

While I took all this in, *Henderson* was busy moving alongside its designated pier space. Boatswains were busy casting weighted "throw lines" to sailors on shore. To the shore-end of the throw line, a huge "hawser," or rope, perhaps six inches in diameter, was tied. Then, parties of men on shore and those on shipboard strained and heaved, pulling each hawser on board, where each was secured to the ship's deck winches. The winches were then activated and slowly drew *Henderson* close alongside of the pier. Now securely berthed, "shore power" was brought on board and hooked into the ship's systems: providing electricity, fresh water, salt water, steam, and air. *Henderson's* boilers and engines were shut down and all shipboard power secured. Next, a small crane approached and delivered a gangway leading from *Henderson's* mid deck to the pier.

# A Warm Welcome

As I stood on deck, idly looking down at the pier activity, I noticed an obviously important, Navy sedan parked near the newly-placed gangway. It had a flagstaff both front and rear, with flags rolled and covered in place. When the owner was present, the flags would be unfurled and the officer thus identified. The driver sat casually behind the steering wheel, and another Navy enlisted man stood beside the vehicle. As soon as the gangway was installed, this second person mounted it and walked on board. He reported to the officer of the deck, saluted, and engaged in conversation. The "OD" listened, summoned a ship's bosun, and gave instructions. The bosun, having received his instructions, turned away and began shouting my name – and for me to report to the gangway "On the double!"

"You're going ashore, now!" he roared, and kept on roaring: "Your gear has been sent for and will be brought to you. Only you are not to leave this pier; do you understand? A bus is being sent for all fifteen of you civilians to be taken to the Labor Board, and you're gonna be on that bus." I was sure we would be.

At age nineteen, I was totally unaware of the protocol being violated by my early exit from the *Henderson*. The bosun summed it up for me: "I don't know who the hell you are, mister. The very idea of the Flag Yeoman of the Commander in Chief, Pacific Fleet, on board telling our skipper that you are going ashore now, ahead of everyone else – even the Commanding Officer of the Fourth Defense Battalion! The very idea!"

I walked alone down the gangplank, to be greeted at the foot by my brother Brand, "Flag Yeoman of the Commander In Chief of the entire Pacific Fleet!" His rating and position would compare to that of "Executive Secretary to the President and Chairman of the Board" of the nation's greatest corporation. No wonder the reaction when he appeared at the head of the gangway and addressed himself to the officer of the deck!

Brand greeted me warmly, welcomed me to Hawaii, and wrote a note giving me his title, address, and how to reach him by phone. We agreed to get in touch as soon as possible so he could provide a personal tour of the island of Oahu and the city of Honolulu.

Word of the incident at the pier and my removal from the ship arrived at the Labor Board, even before the bus with its fifteen civilian passengers. The bus was met by the Industrial Relations Officer himself, a full commander U.S. Navy. The chief, who was our shepherd on the trip, delivered us. He saw me off first in line, to receive a firm handshake and welcome from the Industrial Relations Officer. We were shown into a small briefing room, again welcomed to Pearl Harbor, given papers to read and sign, and advised on what was in store for us. Our next stop would be at "Boys Town," the U.S. Navy Cantonment on the seaward side of the road between the Navy Yard and Hickam Field. Here we would be billeted and fed. The next morning, a bus would return us to the Labor Board, and then each receive an escort from our respective shops to our intended workplace.

# A Gentle Inquiry from the IRO

Following our group briefing, I was taken to the office of the Industrial Relations Officer. Seating me and making me at ease, the commander visited awhile and, at one point, asked me what had brought me to Pearl Harbor. I explained that I was halfway through college and needed to work and save my earnings for my final years. I'd decided that a job as far away from home as possible would enable me to save rather than spend. The commander listened quietly, agreed with my plan, and then advised me not to be surprised at the length of time between my arriving at Pearl Harbor and my eventual return to college. At some point here, I was asked to stand and face the flag, raise my right hand, and give my oath of allegiance to the flag, the Government of the United States, and the U.S. Navy! "Hell," I thought, "this is just like enlisting in the service!"

Casually, the commander raised the point of the admiral's sedan, driver, and flag yeoman being at dockside, and was interested to learn that the flag yeoman was my oldest brother, Brand. Another handshake, and he told me to contact him personally at any time. He also passed along his business card – a short note written to me across the front – and escorted me to the waiting bus, already loaded save myself. *Henderson's* boatswain was still on board, as well as a new chief petty officer from Boys Town. The bus started up, the "IRO" waved, and we were off to our new living quarters.

# Chapter 2.

# First Week at the Shipyard

Figure 3. "Boys Town" (Personal Photo)

## Settling In at the Navy Cantonment

The Navy Cantonment was just beyond the main gate of the Navy Yard and consisted of a cluster of one-story, gable-roofed, barrack-like buildings built of frame and plywood. They were on pilings about two feet above ground level and were stained green. Instead of windows, the upper third of wall space was completely open, save for screens. Inside, each building had a central hallway leading from the back door to the front door with small rooms off to both sides. Each room was large enough for two single cots and two narrow, metal wall lockers. My room already had one occupant, identified as "G. Herman."

When I met him, George turned out to be a tall, lanky, handsome Jewish fellow from New York. George had served a hitch with the U.S. Army in Hawaii, and was now a welder at the Shipyard. Before long, he intended to return to New York and open a shoe store of his own. Toward this end, he saved as much of his earnings as possible.

The cantonment mess hall was provisioned by the Navy and staffed with Navy enlisted personnel. Our board and room expense would include breakfast, dinner, and a packaged lunch – all one wanted, mind you, but no wasting of food allowed. Laundry was collected weekly and returned two days later. Ship service stores were open to us when we presented our Navy identification. Navy work clothes were available to us, including shoes and socks. Thus dressed, we looked exactly as the Navy men, except that we wore no identifying chevrons or ratings, and wore no Navy "white hats." The prices were very reasonable.

Transportation between the cantonment and the shipyard was by "cattle car" – a string of long, goose-neck, fifth-wheel trailers pulled by a Navy truck. There was no charge for transportation.

I stowed my belongings in my metal locker, and then enjoyed my first freshwater shower since leaving California. I so appreciated the soapsuds and lather, and the resulting clean, slippery feeling which a saltwater rinse could just not provide! Afterwards, I had a good Navy supper, visited a bit with George when he arrived, and settled in for the night.

# First Day: Reporting to Shop 71

Next morning before daylight, I was awakened by a boatswain who was striding between the buildings shouting as only a chief boatswain can: "Up all hands! Breakfast in fifteen minutes." Our being civilians, he gave us a "gentler treatment" – his language polite. His announcement meant that we had fifteen minutes to do whatever we would, dress for work, and arrive at the mess hall. There, hunger was satisfied, a lunch collected, and the cattle car buses boarded for the short run over to the Navy Yard. At the gate, Marine sentries boarded the bus and checked each individual's pass before allowing the bus to enter the vast, heavily-secured area which comprised the Navy Yard and harbor.

Most of the shipyard workers did not reside at Boys Town. They arrived from all directions, but always on the Oahu Railroad; it was built on narrow-gage track and pulled by tiny steam-locomotives hauling only a string of open cattle cars. Each car was filled to overflowing with workmen. The outside walls were covered with late-comers hanging on to all spaces available. You could not see a vestige of the car's structure for all the commuters covering it up!

For me, it was back to the Labor Board, but only long enough to report in and for my shop to be called to collect their new worker. That is when I met Willie Watson, the head civilian and the foreman of the Labor Shop, Shop 71. Willie was middle-aged, friendly, and a bit curious about his new man who had arrived under unusual circumstances the previous day. He shook hands with me and visited comfortably as we walked the distance from the Labor Board to Shop 71. There I was shown the time-clock station, clocked in on the timecard bearing my name and number, turned over to my "snapper" (the lowest level of supervisor), and sent off to my first day of work.

## Cleaning Up "The Greek's"

What a day! The small crew to which I was assigned were mostly Filipino – actually, *all* Filipino, except for myself. We spent the day at "The Greek's." The Greek had a franchise with the Navy, allowing him possession of a fair-sized, one-story building within the Navy Yard, fitted out as a cafeteria. At this point in time, the Navy was in the process of putting the Greek out of business and taking the facility over for themselves. Our job was to dispose of all food stuff on the premises.

13

As we worked, I marveled that customers survived after partaking the Greek's bill of fare! The place was absolutely filled with unfit food. We put it all into large trash bins: frozen food of all kinds, dry ingredients complete with weevils and worse, liquids, condiments, fresh meat (much of which was beginning to spoil) and vegetables somewhat unrecognizable. Over all the food piled in the bins, we poured Navy diesel fuel, to make certain that none of it made the way homeward on the "Pineapple Express" that evening.

It took a couple of days to evacuate the premises, which then received a thorough scrubbing, painting, and new flooring. Only then did the Navy begin to move their own equipment into place: new refrigerators, new freezers, all new ranges and ovens, new scullery, mess tables, even a new nickelodeon. Actually, there were two, and, as I recall, each had only two records: "Elmer's Tune" was one and something like "Tonight We Love," was the other. Sailors kept popping nickels into these machines, and that was all one ever heard – over and over and over!

# A Great Crew

Following the job at the Greek's, I was given a group of eight to ten Filipino men with myself in charge. All were two-or-more times my age; all good-humored and ready to laugh at anything. Each was quite ready also to tell all about himself. They laughed hard, and they worked hard and well. Each soon told me that he was a "Filipino" and that I was a "Haolesonofabitch." This with much laughter, of course. I learned that on Oahu – or anywhere else in Hawaii for that matter – if you are Caucasian, you are not a "son of a bitch." You are a "haolesonofabitch," and that the term is not hyphenated: it is all one word. No offense given when so addressed with laughter, and no offense taken. That's just the way it was on the islands where "haole" was Hawaiian for "white."

The older Filipino men had already completed twenty years of active Navy service and were now receiving their retirement pensions. Their job at the Navy Yard allowed them to still feel close to the Navy, and they had their shipyard pay in addition to their pension: an obvious good deal for both them and the Navy.

I guess that I was made boss because of my educational background. No one of my crew seemed to resent my position. We worked hard together, and they cracked jokes and laughed at them throughout the workday.

We finished our first job - scraping the hull of a large barge - and started on the hull of a second barge before the end of the first week. The decomposing marine life, which we swept up and dumped into disposal containers at the end of each day, provided an odor all its own, and helped me not to miss the odors of decay experienced while cleaning out the Greek cafeteria.

When payday came around, everyone except me received a paycheck, being that the Navy always paid two weeks behind the period worked. Thus, the Filipino men of my crew got another laugh, because I was still working for nothing!

Figure 4. Pearl Harbor circa 1940. US Navy Photo NH 54301

# Saturday at the Harbor & Navy Yard: December 6th

Saturday and Sunday were overtime days; and since nothing special demanded our services, those two days belonged to me. Brand had planned to meet me early Sunday morning at the pierside of the battleship *Pennsylvania*. For that reason, I spent Saturday checking out the shipyard. Wearing my blue, Navy-regulation work clothes, and with my shipyard badge clearly visible, I was allowed to walk at will along the waterfront and throughout the yard unchallenged by Marine sentries posted pierside of every ship mooring.

I spent considerable time at Dry Dock No. 1 where *Pennsylvania* and the destroyers, *Cassin* and *Downes*, rested. I had never seen ships in dry dock before, and found it interesting how the huge, concrete blocks were placed in rows. A central row beneath the keel consisted of blocks some six feet in cube with large wooden caps, spaced about ten feet apart. On each side in an arc, outlining the underwater curve of the hull, were two additional rows of blocks with timber caps, also spaced some ten feet apart. This arrangement allowed for cleaning of the underwater portion of the hull, repair, and repainting. The next docking would place the blocks so that the portions missed this time received attention on the next occasion. Looking down, I was amazed at the tremendous size of the underwater portion of the great battleships.

The Navy Yard was a huge facility with eight or nine battleships at anchor or at dry dock. In addition to these massive ships, there were great and impressive battle cruisers and many destroyers, along with a seaplane tender, a minelayer mothership, several minelayers and minesweepers, Navy tugs, tankers, and oilers.

Next to Dry Dock No. 1 was the new dry dock which seemed completed except for the bottom. There was a network of large, steel reinforcing bars partially in place. When this was completed, the concrete floor would be poured, leaving the dry dock finished and ready for use. This new dry dock was wider, deeper, and longer still than the No. 1 dry dock containing *Pennsylvania*.

Further along, I stopped to view the *Shaw*. This destroyer was resting completely out of the water and above the water of the harbor. I can't recall if she was resting in a "marine railway" or in a "floating dry dock," but either would lift her completely above water. Looking up at the ship like this, instead of down at those in dry dock, gave a completely different perspective of the ship and the operations.

A short distance away in the harbor, lay Ford Island with its huge airplane hangars and concrete slopes leading down into the water. These slopes enabled seaplanes landing on the harbor's water to taxi up and out to the hangars or to parking strips ashore. The shoreline of the island was filled with these amphibious planes, lying quietly at rest until Monday morning when they would be flying off the water again on seaward patrols.

An extra-large pier began at the water end of the dry dock in which *Pennsylvania* rested. This pier extended out into the harbor waters and had several ships tied up on both sides. At the water end of the pier stood the hammerhead crane, so called because it looked like an upended, straight-clawed carpenters hammer. It was the first structure which anyone coming into the harbor saw, and it towered over everything else. An aircraft carrier looked small in comparison when moored alongside – with the crane lifting the radar antennae and holding what would become part of the ship's highest superstructure in place as workmen assembled and welded it onto the carrier. The control tower of the crane formed the traveling-end of the crane. This entire top part of the crane could be rotated in a full circle while the length of the claw enabled it to provide service over a considerable range. The hammerhead was also used to lift tugs, barges, and smaller craft completely out of the water, and place them on long, sturdy trailers. These could be towed to work areas well away from the precious waterfront.

Especially, I was taken by the "marine railway." The marine railway consisted of extra-heavy, steel railroad track spaced widely apart and embedded in a heavy concrete slab. The rails went out into the harbor and well below the surface as an inclined plane. They ended above the water near a huge, mechanical windlass with anchor-chain connecting to the railway sled. Large, concrete dock-cubes were put in place in three lines on top of a powerful sled riding on the railway. The first line lay directly beneath the keel. The second and third lines, outboard of this on either side, traced the curve of the ship's bottom sides – a space of fifteen feet or so between each block. When the ship was placed carefully over these blocks, the railway was activated to pull the sled and the cradled ship out of the water and onto the shore. There, workmen had access to the hull as if it had been in dry dock.

The shop buildings were immense: long, wide, and high with huge, horizontal-sliding doors. The interiors were open and multi-storied – perhaps six stories high. Along the side walls were balconies for office space, layout rooms, and pre-assembly rooms, all of which were easily serviced by the huge bridge cranes as wide as the building.

The orderliness and cleanliness of the shipyard was amazing, with a planned space for everything and an understood duty for everyone. It seemed that lost motion didn't even exist, and the efficiency of the shipyard was evident everywhere. I was very impressed, as well I should be.

When I arrived at Pearl Harbor, the civilian workforce was small. The yard had previously existed to perform only temporary work on vessels, preparing them for return to a West Coast shipyard and complete reconditioning. Only a few months earlier, the Pacific Fleet had been moved, temporarily, it was thought, from the West Coast to Hawaii. Not long afterwards, the relocation was made permanent, and the need to expand the workforce became imperative. It was this expansion which had caught me up, and which now found me living at Boys Town and working at Pearl Harbor.

## War with Japan Expected Soon

Saturday noontime, I lunched at the shipyard cafeteria. It was well-filled with Navy enlisted men who accepted me as one of their own. Mostly, I listened to their exchanges of information and rumors. Without exception, the subject was "**WAR**" and more specifically, war with Japan. This, they said, would surely come soon, and would be instigated by the Japanese. They were absolutely certain of what they were saying. They expressed no fear, no hesitancy, and showed a calmness about the forthcoming situation. They were all so sure.

I asked how they could be so certain. Surprised, eyes turned to me and various voices answered: "You are obviously very new to the Island. Most of us have been here for months and it is common knowledge. There are Japanese spies all over. The FBI and the Office of Naval Intelligence are watching, making notes, and identifying as many key enemy-agents as possible. Even so, there is no law against sitting on a hill overlooking the harbor and observing and making sketches of installations and equipment and ships; no law against identifying ships and stations, airfields and dispersal patterns of planes on the ground. Yes, we know that war is coming, and soon. We just don't know where they will strike first or when it will happen – but it will be soon."

I spent the afternoon continuing on my walk about the shipyard and through some of the bigger shops. No one challenged my business in being there. Toward evening, I walked to the Labor Board just inside the main gate and caught a cattle car directly to Boys Town. My evening meal was at the Navy mess hall, after which I made my way to my barrack room for towel and soap to shower and shave. That evening, I sat and wrote a letter home. In part it said, "War is coming, and coming soon. That is all I can write about it for now." Then I lay down to sleep after a long day's walk.

# Chapter 3.
# December 7th and Aftermath: War

## Witnessing the Surprise Attack: Sunday Morning

Awaking early Sunday morning, I had breakfast at Boys Town and then boarded a cattle car bus for the short ride to the Navy Yard. My brother, Brand, had invited me for a tour of his ship. Once inside the main gate, I walked the brief distance to where the battleship *Pennsylvania* rested in dry dock and waited alongside for Brand's arrival. On board the *Pennsylvania*, the ship's band had already assembled on the rear deck awaiting 08:00: the time the huge Stars and Stripes would be raised to their accompaniment of the National Anthem.

Figure 5. Japanese Navy carrier bomber during the attack. US Navy Photo 80-G-32908

Standing nearby, I continued taking in the quiet and orderly activities. Casually, I noticed several single-engine planes in silhouette coming on a glide path toward the harbor. Not too far distant from these, I saw still more planes of another flight. Their outline was dark and unrecognizable. Then explosions began – explosions all around me! The planes would pull up from where they had been low over the water, circle, and come in again. More were joining them! As they pulled up and circled, their colors became visible. The red ball became easily recognized on fuselage and wing. These were Jap planes! They were making torpedo runs, bombing runs – strafing runs! The Japs were attacking Pearl Harbor, for God's sake!

Smoke began rising: small at first, but rapidly increasing into huge, billowing clouds from explosive detonations deep within stricken ships. Fuel oil from ruptured ships' tanks began covering the surface of the harbor's clear waters. Then fire began spreading on the floating fuel.

At first I just stood there, mouth wide open, staring, in total disbelief. Flying metal, bomb fragments, bullets all around, bouncing like hailstones off the concrete. It was like standing in the middle of a hailstorm in North Dakota! I backed against a nearby structure (probably an electric substation), stood still, and watched.

A bomb hit *Pennsylvania* on the portside seaplane crane. The explosion was great, and I could feel the compressed air from the concussion's blast squeeze my head like the jaws of a vice. My hearing deadened and my ears began to ring. A second bomb went directly down the smokestack of one of the destroyers directly ahead of the *Pennsylvania* in the dry dock. Ship's steel ripped apart from the blast and flew everywhere, some bouncing along the concrete pier in landing. Internal fires broke out in both destroyers, and more smoke clouds were added to the mass of clouds already forming over the stricken harbor.

Jap planes were still everywhere making bomb, bullet, and torpedo attacks. Looking over toward Boys Town, I could see other Jap planes delivering similar attacks to Hickam Field hangars and the airplanes lined up in parade-fashion on the ground!

Figure 6. View from Pier 1010, looking toward the Pearl Harbor Navy Yard's dry docks. In the foreground is the capsized *USS Oglala* with *USS Helena* further down the pier, at left. Beyond *Helena* is Dry Dock No. 1 with *USS Pennsylvania* and the burning destroyers *Cassin* and *Downes*.
US Navy Photo 80-G-474789

One torpedo went under the *Oglala* striking the new cruiser, *Helena*. The explosion was tremendous. *Oglala* began turning completely over in the water just across the pier from *Pennsylvania* while I was still standing in between.

Figure 7. *USS Arizona* sunk and burning furiously, 7 December 1941. At left, men on the stern of *USS Tennessee* are playing fire hoses on the water to force burning oil away from their ship. US Navy Photo 80-G-19942

I saw, heard, and felt explosions from the *Arizona* as she was hit again and again. The battleship *Arizona* was 608 feet long, 97 feet wide and about 35,000 tons heavy. I have not words to describe the magnitude of the explosions. Then, even as I watched, Arizona lifted up, unbelievably, from the water, forward mast tilted crazily to one side. She slowly sank, finally resting on the bottom of the harbor. The waterline to Ford Island was crushed beneath her bulk, leaving Ford Island without this desperately-needed resource to fight the conflagrations. From ships afire and oil-coated water ablaze, black and grey smoke was low on the water and rising high in the air.

Ship's boats and small craft began appearing all over the harbor. Each was working independently, going everywhere, pulling struggling swimmers and others horribly injured out of the oily, flaming water, taking them ashore where they were left while the boat crews returned again and again into the harbor for more casualties blackened with fuel oil, clothing saturated, gooey, slippery, and heavy. In this unbelievable chaos, a few boats were recognizable as being used by Navy photographers engaged in their official duty of recording the escalating disaster at Pearl Harbor.

With my back against the concrete substructure, facing the onslaught, I continued to stand and watch the attack as it unfolded, making no effort to seek cover or protect myself, mesmerized by the scenes, all too much to take in or to fully comprehend! I couldn't believe it! Finally, I had seen enough to comprehend the situation. I turned and, staying close to the shop walls, ran the short distance to my home shop in the Navy Yard. Once inside and sheltered from view of the continuing attack, I felt a little safer – although protected only by thin, corrugated metal walls. I hurried to my locker, got into dungarees, and reported myself present and available. Because it was early morning, I was one of the few to assemble, and was promptly sent out as part of a small rescue party.

## During the Attack

As a small group, we moved along the waterfront and piers collecting men who had just been left ashore by the rescue boats and whose bodies and clothing were streaked and saturated with harbor oil. We assisted them to the nearby dispensary, conveniently located midway along the waterfront. There we left them outside on the pavement for attention by corpsmen, nurses, and physicians. Those beyond assistance, and there were many, were moved to another location and left for others to pick up.

I have no memory of how long we labored while the attack continued. Much later, I learned that the attack involved 420 enemy planes, lasted for something over two hours, and was supported by the six newest aircraft carriers of the Jap Navy. I have no recollection of stopping for even a drink of water or a bite of food, and too soon I was smeared like all the rest with fuel oil, salt water, and blood.

Many men were beyond assistance, and sometimes there were only body parts: a trouser leg containing part of a blown-off leg, a shirt with a severed arm remaining. There were bodies with catastrophic wounds, some burned beyond any hope of recognition. The scene was appalling. Some of the Labor Shop men, who could not bear the rescue work assignment, were put to work elsewhere. I remained part of the original crew and continued picking up survivors and getting them to the dispensary triage area which now contained a line of trucks and ambulances loading and moving the injured on to medical facilities beyond the shipyard.

Figure 8. *USS Maryland* at Berth F-5, with men working on the capsized hull of *USS Oklahoma* alongside, during or immediately after the Japanese attack. US Navy Photo NH83065

*Oklahoma*, after taking many hits, slowly began turning over as crewmen abandoned ship, diving or sliding into the water. Finally, *Oklahoma* rested upside down, her huge side-propeller sticking up above the oil-blackened and flame-licked water.

By now, Pearl Harbor was a hell pit of smoke: grey, brown, white, lemon-yellow, black, and all acrid and foul. Flaming, mushrooming billows were erupting skyward, folding in and then opening out, creating a mass of storm clouds – and predicting the horrors to come.

Figure 9. *USS Nevada* headed down channel past the Navy Yard's 1010 Dock, under Japanese air attack during her sortie from Battleship Row. Photographed from Ford Island.   US Navy Photo NH 97397

Out of all this pall came the indescribable sight of the battleship *Nevada* underway and heading into the channel – a hole the size of a house in her bow and torn flag waving defiantly off her stern – trying for the open sea. Like crows after an ear of corn, the Jap planes swarmed after her, intent on stopping her great mass and sinking her in place. This would totally block the channel opening to the sea.

Coming in close alongside, the captain of the destroyer *Allen* screamed across to *Nevada*: "CINCPAC orders you to beach your ship and keep the channel clear." He screamed himself hoarse until finally heard. *Nevada* acknowledged, changed course, and successfully ground to a halt as ordered – all the while being battered and taking casualties from enemy aircraft.

# Flooding the Dry Dock

There was a new, nearly-completed dry dock which was likely to be an important target for the enemy. The dry-dock structure was complete, except for placing the reinforcing steel and pouring the massive, concrete floor. It was decided that flooding the dry dock full would make it much harder to destroy. Only a few civilians had ever been in the structure, and no one knew their whereabouts.

Three of us were pulled out of our crew. We were to open one of the flooding gates of the dry dock. Why they picked me, God only knows. I had never been in a dry dock and had no idea how it operated. Someone gave a verbal description of the descending stairwell and of the steel, watertight doors which had to be "undogged" to open and then properly closed and "dogged" behind us to be watertight. I was briefed on what the manual control room looked like fifty feet below, given a sketch of manual levers to release, and told how to turn the four-foot-diameter steel wheel. This would open one of the floodgates and allow full flow of seawater into the tunnel and thence into the dry dock.

No electric power was available; so with powerful battery lights in hand, we proceeded down the enclosed stairwell and into the small, compact control room. As instructions dictated, the proper levers were released, others engaged, and the large handwheel slowly turned to open the floodgate. I could feel and hear the seawater entering. It took a lot of wheel-turns to fully open the gate (which was probably six feet high and four feet wide). Considering the ocean-pressure, it opened relatively easily with two men bending to the task as the third held the battery-powered lanterns. We stayed below quite some time. When satisfied that our job was done, we reversed our way, opening and closing the steel watertight-doors as we went.

My next solid recollection concerns what happened after dark. By that time, I had cleaned up with solvent, soap, and hot water and changed into dry clothing. Galleys of serviceable ships were now open and fully manned around-the-clock. Battleships under normal conditions fed over a thousand men each day. Now they prepared to feed anyone, military and civilian, who came aboard. Heavy cruisers operated their galleys in similar manner and even destroyers had coffee and sandwiches at all times for anyone going through the chow line.

# Expectations of Another Attack

Marine sentries were everywhere: each armed with rifle and fixed bayonet, each rifle fully-loaded and ready. Unknown to us at the time, all military had been given the order: "If action is required, shoot to kill."

Figure 10. The wrecked destroyers *USS Downes* and *USS Cassin* in Dry Dock 1 at the Pearl Harbor Navy Yard, soon after the end of the Japanese air attack. *Cassin* has capsized against *Downes*. *USS Pennsylvania* is astern, occupying the rest of the dry dock. US Navy Photo 80-G-19943.

I recall sentries at Dry Dock No. 1 where two destroyers, the *Cassins* and *Downes*, were still burning. Other than fires, the Navy Yard was without light. Vehicles moved about with tiny, blue lights silhouetting their outline. Flashlights also had a dim, blue lens giving almost no illumination. Clearly, I remember one sentry observing an open flame, probably from an unthinking person lighting a smoke. "Put out that light!" the sentry had shouted. Next, he raised his rifle and shot at the light. It instantly disappeared. There was continual fear of additional fires. Marines were jumpy and took no threatening actions from anyone.

Everyone, military and civilian, realized how totally vulnerable the islands were to enemy attack. It was also assumed that the Jap planes would return later that day and night, then follow up with a land invasion in force probably the next day, 8 December. Army units were dispersed strategically all over the island of Oahu, equipped with all field gear to enable them to remain away from garrison support. Navy and Marine Corps were dispersed in similar manner around Navy and Marine Corps installations.

Sunday afternoon, CINCPAC (Commander in Chief, Pacific Command) was alerted that a flight of carrier planes would be arriving after dark preceding the arrival of one of our carriers. Word of the arrivals was passed along with the instructions: "Hold your fire." Unfortunately, when detected on radar, the incoming flight was misinterpreted as the advance flight of the anticipated second-attack. As single-engine planes came in low over the harbor, all available weapons engaged! To me on the ground in the midst of this activity, it was beyond description! I was right in the center under a sky of gunfire, closing in from all around me like the spokes of an open umbrella. The sky was ablaze from weapons that ringed the harbor and from ships – all firing overhead at the incoming planes. The light from bursting, heavy anti-aircraft fire; the phosphorescent brilliance of tracer-ammunition from light and large machine guns; and the tracer-fire from rifles illuminated the airspace above the harbor nearly as bright as day.

One plane turned its lights on and flew directly into the faces of ground gunners; it successfully flared and landed on the strip at Ford Island. Another burst into flames and the pilot could be seen coming earthward in his parachute. The next day, we learned that the flight was made up of six carrier planes from *USS Enterprise* arriving ahead of their mothership. Through this awful and awesome concentration, three of the six pilots had survived!

The hangars at Ford Island continued to burn. Battleship *California*, when hit, had flooded evenly, allowing it to settle in the muddy harbor bottom without capsizing. Oil-fed fires raged on *California* for over three days. I don't recall how long *Arizona* continued to burn.

As soon as it was feasible, intense efforts were begun to rescue men who were trapped below decks on many of the ships. The courage, determination, and ingenuity of those involved – both rescuers and those trapped – resulted in many lives saved.

# Afterward:
# Cleaning the Ship Interior

Figure 11. *USS California* had been sunk as a result of the attack and was refloated on 24 March 1942. This photo was taken just after she was placed in the Navy Yard's Dry Dock No. Two, 9 April 1942.
US Navy Photo NH 64483

I don't recall just when, but one of the sunken ships was raised and brought into dry dock where the flooded interior was completely drained of seawater. During the interim between the

Pearl Harbor attack and the docking, the flesh from the bodies of entombed sailors had decomposed, and the body fat had covered the surface of the enclosed water. In dry dock, as the water level was pumped down, this conglomeration of material followed and coated every interior surface until it was thick and heavy with the substance.

Our first job was to wipe…and steam…and wash…and wipe again and…*again* all accessible surfaces. The task was indescribable, and the odors beyond one's imagination! So many workers absolutely could not accommodate to the task and environment. Those of us who could, stuck with it, perhaps as much out of recognition of the sacrifice made by those who had previously occupied these spaces as for any other reason.

This was, without a doubt, the most difficult task I ever performed in my life, and I grew to hate the Jap for what they were: not animals, for animals have a dignity – but as calculating savages who let nothing stand in their way, and who entertained themselves with cruelty. For the rest of the war it was "get-even-time" for me; I never tortured or maimed, but never hesitated to shoot first and shoot to kill. I always knew with the Jap, it was either him or me; and I early-on made up my mind never to be taken prisoner under any circumstance. I stayed to complete the cleaning of one ship. We had done all we could, but the odor was never truly gone. Then I asked for and received a transfer from the Labor Shop to the Welding Shop.

# Welding

Because of the shortage of welders, the shop was accepting unskilled applicants for on-the-job training. The Welding Shop and the Shipfitter Shop functioned as a single unit. Shipfitters were tradesmen who traced outlines onto the surface of steel beams, sheets, and plates. "Burners," men using acetylene torches, cut the steel as outlined. "Chippers" followed with air-powered tools, removing scale and rough edges. Then the welders took over putting the pieces together and welding them together with watertight welds. Beams, and often timbers, were then attached. The completed fabrication was lifted by huge, overhead bridge cranes, placed on long trailers, and removed from the shop to the waiting vessel.

My first assignment was on the "welding slab," which was raised a couple of feet off the shop floor on steel legs. This steel deck was about six inches thick and like a checkerboard, only the "black squares" in this case were steel and the "red squares" were complete openings through the plate. The area of each was about four inches by four inches.

Here I learned how to power up and to adjust the arc welding machine, which welding rod was needed for a given purpose, and what diameter of rod to use for that job. Next, I learned how to "strike an arc" by lightly brushing the tip of the rod across the steel surface being worked on, and how to flow the molten steel along the edges of the plates being welded. This caused all adjacent surfaces to meld and flow together, eventually cooling into solid steel. The process took concentration, touch, skill, and patience. Learning required methodical practice. My supervisor was an old-timer and showed a lot of concern that we were sufficiently skilled before putting us on our own.

The Shipfitter Welding Shop was one of the largest structures in the Navy Yard. The main shop was one large open-area: four-stories high and the full length of the building. Up near the ceiling on each side was a single, heavy crane-rail running the full length of the building; and across its width were three or four huge "bridge cranes." Below, along the side walls at the first-floor level, were "jib cranes," which provided lifting capability to machinery. The huge cranes, alone and in tandem, were used to raise massive assemblies and carry them out the expansive main doors. From there, two mobile cranes would maneuver the "lift" onto a trailer. The load would then be hauled to the waterfront and the awaiting floating crane.

On each side of the shop, running the full length of the building, were balcony enclosures of "layout rooms" and subassembly areas. The building actually housed a complete manufacturing facility.

I practiced until I could make a watertight weld. Only then, I was assigned below decks on one of the old World War One destroyers. We were to weld bricks of steel along the keel to provide ballast at the proper places in the ship's bottom. The steel in these hulls had not been well-preserved, and it was easy to burn a hole right through the steel, allowing seawater to spout up and in. I quickly learned how to weld any new holes closed again. Likewise, the decks were all so thin and rusty, that it was easy to put one's boot right through the deck when walking about. These destroyers, now tied up alongside one of the piers, had been in reserve anchorage: probably in San Francisco Bay since shortly after our first World War. They had rested there with little or no maintenance over the years. Now they were being remodeled, overhauled, repaired, and made ready for service.

The deck and hull plates of my ship (I forget the name or number) received early attention, as no one wanted to land on the deck below. Shipfitters, burners, chippers, welders, riggers, and crane operators worked as a team: identifying the bad plates, marking them, cutting out and removing the corroded materials, replacing them with new steel, and welding the structure anew. Any bottom plates in unsound condition would be removed and replaced later, when the ship was in dry dock.

Working in the ship's "double-bottom," or "bilge," we placed the "engineered ballast" of cast-iron weights. This was difficult, as the work space was low and cramped, the weights were heavy, and the air was smoky and foul; but I was learning and happy to be productive. As my skill increased, I was assigned to a team of shipfitters and welders. Thereafter, we worked on whatever fabrication or installation job was on hand that day.

# Refloating and Repairing the Ships

Figure 12.
*USS California*: Refloating operations while the ship was under salvage at Pearl Harbor on 30 March 1942. Note the cofferdam installed along her port bow and forward turrets with guns removed.
US Navy Photo NH 55036

One project was making "cofferdams" to be placed over any huge holes in ships' hulls. The process was like applying a Band-Aid over a wound, only in this case, placed three feet away from the area damaged. The perimeter was made of I-beams, cut and shaped to the design-contour of the hull at the point of damage. It looked like half of a boat hull. The outer-portion was made of heavy timber and caulked to make it watertight. When ready, one would be taken from the shop using two powerful bridge-cranes, placed on large trailers, taken to the waterfront, and loaded onto a barge. The barge delivered it to a sunken ship. There, the freshly-fabricated "half-hull" was lifted by a huge floating-crane and lowered into the water as close to the damage as possible. It was further positioned by crane and tugboat to fit over the massive hole in the ship's hull. Pressure from the tug kept it there while welders, working underwater, fabricated it into place.

Underwater welding is done inside a large air bubble. The welder would go underwater using a diver's suit. When in place to work, a continuous, large air-bubble was formed using compressed-air directed through an air hose. Inside this dry bubble, the welder would strike his arc and proceed to weld! A highly sophisticated and technical operation indeed!

Figure 13. Pumping out the ship (*USS California*) after installation of a cofferdam along her bow's port side, while she was under salvage at Pearl Harbor on 27 February 1942. US Navy Photo NH 55034

With the cofferdam welded in place, large pumps were activated to begin pumping water from inside the sunken craft. As flotation began, the ship would roll, seeking its balance, and slowly begin to make its way back to the surface! Now it could be taken by Navy tugs to an available dry dock where it was lowered onto "keel blocks" set in a special pattern to fit the ship's size and shape. Finally, vast quantities of water, which had been contained within the ship, would pour from the still-leaking hull into the dry dock, leaving the ship's interior coated with oil, muck, body fat, and a mess and odor beyond description.

At this point, the cofferdam could be removed and the cutting away of damaged parts begun in preparation for replacement by new materials being fabricated in the shipfitter shop. Once the hull and structure had been repaired, the ship could be taken from dry dock to a pier for all other work required to make it capable of steaming to Mare Island or Bremerton for full reconstruction. Then another sunken ship would be raised for the beginning of its restoration! It was amazing how a "destroyed and dead" ship could be brought back to full, serviceable life!

# Gambling

My paychecks piled up and were uncashed until late January when I took them to the RCA cable office located at the credit union in the shipyard. There, I turned them in for a money cable, which RCA delivered to my mother in Ohio. Further collections of checks were similarly sent by way of RCA money cable. Checks were large, especially for 1941 and 1942. Two-and-a-half days of work completed a forty-hour week. The rest of the time became "time-and-a-half," except Sundays and holidays; they were "double time-and-a-quarter." Years later, I received a letter from the Navy stating that my pay at that time was 500 dollars a week.

With the advent of large paychecks came the inevitable invasion of gamblers as well. The shipyard was expanding its civilian workforce to more than double its former size, and workers were arriving from everywhere "Stateside." Many came only for the opportunity to gamble.

The gamblers mostly evaded reporting for work, and remained at Boys Town where they kept gambling tables going day and night. Many workmen kept their money in heavy, black, cardboard shell-cases about three inches in diameter and eighteen inches long. How much was crammed into a shell-case? No one had any idea. In their free time, some took their shell-case with them to Honolulu, where they invaded jewelry stores and turned their profits into gems. Others always had their shell-case next to them. I never gambled, but watched now and then in astonishment and disbelief. One young man from Georgia gambled at "red dog," a variety of wild poker, and always managed to lose his paycheck – until May, that is. On Mother's Day, he sent a money cable home with a note: "Dear Mom, Put the check into a bank account. We'll use it to buy a farm when I get home." It was for $25,000!

The Navy chief bosuns knew all that was going on by way of gambling and men staying away from work. They also participated with Navy Criminal Investigation in gathering evidence – even to the point of entering the activity themselves. It was then that, every so often, faces of familiar gamblers disappeared from Boys Town with no explanation. What happened to them, I never knew; but they never returned.

## The Mountain of Fire Bricks

Supervisors in the Shipfitter Shop weren't dealing with gamblers. Their problems were some men who thought that they needed to "rest up"! At one end of the shop's high-bay areas was a mountain of "fire brick" – a ceramic insulation material, being stored until needed for the relining of ships' boilers. The blocks protected the boilers from the super-high internal temperatures generated when burning fuel oil to produce the high-pressure steam needed to power the ships' steam-turbine propulsion systems.

Fire brick in storage was protected by layers of straw, and became a favored nesting place for scorpions. The fire brick mountain was also a favorite nesting place for "goldbricking" workmen who crawled up to grab a bit of sleep.

To find these slackers, supervisors would fill barrels with water, carry them aloft on the big bridge-cranes over the mountain, and spill the content on sleepers below – successfully flushing them out of their comfortable resting spots. Scorpions contributed as well! Every so often, the overhead would rattle with the scream of a slumbering workman who, having rolled over on a scorpion, had been rudely awakened by its prompt and severe sting! The name of the injured then received a check in someone's "black book." Furthermore, he received no sympathy from the dispensary when he reported for treatment. Scorpion stings and freshwater showers slowed up a large number of the loafers, but failed to halt those more determined. Eventually, bad work-records resulted in workmen being dismissed from the shipyard and vacated from Boys Town.

Figure 14. Japanese Type A midget submarine in Fredericksburg, Texas, birthplace of Fleet Admiral Chester W. Nimitz, during a national War Bond tour, circa 1943. (Captured on 8 December 1941 after it unsuccessfully attempted to enter Pearl Harbor during the attack on the previous day). US Navy Photo NH 62816

# An Unusual Submarine Sighting

Following the relief of General Short from command, General Emmons took over as Commanding General of the Army in Hawaii, and also functioned in the dual capacity of Military Governor of the Territory of Hawaii. Complete blackout was enforced from dusk until dawn, with a matching curfew covering the same time frame. During these hours, vehicle lights were restricted to the very dim, blue headlights. The few persons authorized to be out at night and the necessary military and police vehicles were all that moved.

One dark night, a shipyard workman, returning home after his shift had ended, stopped a police vehicle. "Officer," was his first word. "Officer, I just saw a submarine going down the middle of the street towards the pier at Aloha Tower!" The police didn't even stop to smell his breath before taking him in and tossing him into the drunk tank! He was released early next morning, by which time news of the submarine story was all over town. He had been correct in his sighting: The previous night a complete, Jap, miniature submarine, which had been placed on a huge truck-trailer, was moved right down the middle of the street to Aloha Tower. There, it had been loaded on the foredeck of the battleship *California*. Now raised, refloated, and temporarily repaired, *California* was leaving for Mare Island Naval Shipyard in California for complete rebuilding, refitting, and a new life of service. The submarine affixed to her deck was being taken Stateside where, we were told, it would begin a long railroad-tour in promotion of War Bonds sales.

## Stand-Off with Illegal Entrepreneurs: The Red Light District

The "Red Light District" was concentrated in the part of Honolulu closest to the Navy Yard and the ocean front. A cluster of rather large and old two-story homes, which had been rather grand in earlier times, made up the complex. For health reasons, Navy doctors and corpsmen maintained close watch and inspection of the "female entertainers" who occupied the premises and "worked" there. On any given day, a long, single line of servicemen formed, patiently waiting outside for their turn to enter. The going price for the entertainment was two dollars. Each private and seaman was receiving twenty-one dollars per month plus ten percent for overseas duty.

In June 1942, a grateful nation raised this pay to fifty dollars a month, plus the ten percent for overseas duty. Quite naturally, the ladies thought it reasonable to have a pay raise for themselves as well. Their fee promptly went up to four dollars.

44

General Emmons was outraged! He immediately posted military police and shore patrol at each house and allowed no one into or out of the quarters. The main newspaper, the *Honolulu Star*, began running editorials about how "certain female entertainers" were so unpatriotic and greedy that they had doubled the price of their entertainment. Thus, a standoff came about which lasted several days, during which rations inside the barricade became evermore scarce. Finally, a truce was arranged by negotiators: the price returned to the previous rate and General Emmons pulled his military police and shore patrol from the blockade. Thereafter, business resumed the same as before.

## Reconnecting with Brand

Ever since the bombing and without success, I had tried to contact my brother Brand. I had no idea if he was injured during the December 7th attack. It took a month for the letter I wrote to be delivered to him at the sub base across the harbor. He was well and unhurt. In January, he came to see me. Admiral Kimmel was returning to Washington and Brand was to accompany him. It was fifty years later that I learned of his activities. Secretary of Navy, Frank Knox, had arrived in Hawaii on December 11th to learn firsthand as much as possible about what had happened and why. On December 18th, the Roberts Commission was appointed by President Roosevelt; its members arrived December 22nd in Hawaii to investigate and fix responsibility and blame for the disaster. Brand, being flag yeoman to Admiral Kimmel, was fully engaged during both occasions. He never spoke to me of these events. In Washington, Brand was taken into Admiral Leahy's personal staff. In 1943, he was commissioned in the U.S. Navy and began a long career as a line officer, retiring with the rank of commander.

# The *USS Chester*

In one of the early sea battles of 1942, the Raid on Taroa, the heavy cruiser, the *USS Chester*, was badly hit, but able to make it to Pearl Harbor. I was one of the many who worked full time on repair while she was in port. I made many friends among the ship's complement of shipfitters and welders. I liked the ship and the new friendships and spoke with the division officer about joining up as part of the *Chester's* crew. The ship's officers and the men whom I worked with liked the idea. I was to enlist and become welder 3rd class. The problem arose when the officer from the *Chester* met with the Shipyard Industrial Relations officer, who promptly squashed the proposal. I was a civilian yard-worker, he explained. I was essential to the Navy Yard, and everyone might as well forget this idea. *Chester* was put out to sea again, while I remained ashore at my Navy Yard job. Later, when we heard rumors the *USS Chester* had been sunk, I felt very fortunate to have been required to stay behind. The rumors proved untrue. She had been torpedoed, but survived. I never learned what her casualties were until much later after the war: eleven crewmen had been killed, and twelve wounded.

Figure 15.
*USS Chester* off the Mare Island Navy Yard, California, after torpedo damage repairs and overhaul, 2 October 1943.
US Navy Photo 19-N-54656

# Early May: Battle of the Coral Sea

The Coral Sea, located between Guadalcanal and northeastern Australia, saw a huge naval battle early in May 1942, between surface ships of both sides. Each had carriers enabling them to launch devastating air-attacks. The U.S. goal was to halt further southern and westward expansion by the Japs into the Solomon Islands, New Caledonia, New Zealand, and Australia.

In this battle, I believe that the Jap lost 92 aircraft, 1074 men, and an aircraft carrier. The U. S. lost 66 aircraft, a tanker, a destroyer, 543 men, and the aircraft carrier *Lexington*.

Figure 16. Scene on board *USS Yorktown*, shortly after she was hit by three Japanese bombs on 4 June 1942. Taken by Photographer 2nd Class William G. Roy. US Navy Photo 80-G-312018

It was here that the carrier *Yorktown* took a bomb near the control island. It penetrated the flight deck, the hangar deck, the galley below – and was only stopped and exploded by the

47

armored deck fifty feet below. Through all this, *Yorktown* continued landing and launching flights into the ongoing battle.

I learned, when they were back at Pearl Harbor, that when the alert "BATTLE STATIONS" is sounded over the ship's public address system, every man on board buckles into his personal life-preserver, dons his steel helmet, and double-times to his action station. This includes all galley personnel and all ship's administrative personnel as well. Each has a fighting station. When "BATTLE STATIONS" was sounded on board *Lexington*, the ship's canteen was opened, and 10,000 candy bars were issued to its nearly 3,000 crewmen, because – until the battle was secured – the galley would be completely shut down and silent.

Figure 17. *USS Yorktown* in Dry Dock #1 at the Pearl Harbor Navy Yard, 29 May 1942, receiving urgent repairs for damage received in the Battle of the Coral Sea. US Navy Photo 80-G-13065

# Preparing for Midway:
# Repair of the *USS Yorktown*

Now, late in May, the Battle of Midway was shaping up, as the Japanese intended to land troops and take possession of the tiny island. For their part, the Japanese fleet included four heavy and three light aircraft carriers, along with the bulk of the Japanese fleet. The U.S. Navy was throwing everything it had into the battle against them.

On May 27th, the carrier, *Yorktown*, trailing a ten-mile oil slick behind her, succeeded in making her way back from the Coral Sea to Pearl Harbor. Despite the damage sustained, which would require three months to repair in the Shipyard, Admiral Nimitz ordered that she be made ready to join the fleet in three days.

*Yorktown* went into dry dock that same day, complete with fuel on board. Bombs, ammunition, and explosives remained in place. She continued to be re-provisioned with food, water, additional fuel, and ammunition – even as work was being accomplished. This was the exact opposite of the usual procedure where all fuel and explosives would be taken off before the ship was dry-docked.

One thousand four hundred shipyard workmen were brought on board. They labored around-the-clock for 72 hours, without rest or relief, making the ship temporarily ready to rejoin the fleet. I was one of those workmen. We were organized into small crews and given assignments to complete on board. Armed Marine sentries were stationed with each group to provide safety, fire-watch, and security.

Damaged steel plates were cut away and removed, and new materials cut and welded into place. Damaged steel beams were removed and replaced with huge timbers for shoring, bracing, and temporarily strengthening the ship's framework. Electric cables, communication cables, and steam and water lines were held in place near ceilings on metal shelves called "utility trays." Damaged ones were cut away and replaced with new equipment.

We worked so closely together that it was impossible to protect our eyes from "flash burns" when welding. We continued working in spite of the eye injuries we incurred (and which required days of treatment later on to heal). Without being told, each of us knew that if the Japanese won the oncoming Battle of Midway, their next move would be for the control of Oahu and Pearl Harbor.

Navy men from the ship's galley brought sandwiches and lots of coffee to each of us working on board. This food was accepted gratefully and consumed quickly, even as we continued to work. When any of us needed to relieve ourselves, a Marine sentry would leave the team, escort the person to the nearest head, and then right back to the job site. Thus, no one was allowed to wander about the ship and everyone was kept busily occupied.

It seemed unbelievable – even to us: The hull, deck, structure-damage, and utility-damage had been repaired and made strong enough for *Yorktown* to put to sea with the rest of the carrier force leaving for Midway. We worked on board right up to the time she left the harbor, using every minute of our three days.

The *USS Yorktown* departed Saturday, 30th of May, with all signal flags flying from her superstructure. Her flight deck was lined with hundreds of crewmen and the dock was lined with hundreds of yard-workmen who had been part of her history for 72 hours. Thunderous cheers went up as both sides saluted each other, and *Yorktown* departed a safe harbor for the next mighty battle awaiting her.

## A Well-Earned Day of Rest!

Having completed our work on this special carrier, those of us needing attention reported to the dispensary. There, corpsmen and doctors examined our conditions. Ointment was generously applied to the eyes of those of us having experienced "flash burns," and – although it dimmed one's vision temporarily – this was effective in relieving and healing the condition. Tubes of salve were distributed to be used as needed for further relief.

We reported back to the Welding Shop where supervisors called their crews together who had worked on *Yorktown* for days without rest. Each one was given one day off work. Sunday, May 31, 1942 would be my first time-off since 7 December, 1941!

By now, I was skinny, and I was tired – and I wanted to get some rest. Also, I knew exactly what I was going to do next. That Saturday, I returned to Boys Town, took a hot shower, put on clean clothes, enjoyed my first full meal in days, and went to sleep.

With the feeling that the Jap still intended to invade and take Oahu and Pearl Harbor, I concluded it much preferable to be in uniform and armed to fight. Thus it was, next morning, that I changed to my going-to-town clothes, went to the road at Boys Town entrance, and caught the bus which would take me to Schofield Barracks.

Figure 18. Aerial View of Schofield Barracks.
US Army photo reprinted from *The 25th Division and World War 2* (p 14), Cpt. Robert F. Karolevitz, ed., 1946, Army and Navy Publishing Company.

# Chapter 4.
# Goodbye Navy, Hello Army
## May 31, 1942

## 1st Day Off After the Pearl Harbor Attack: Enlisting in the Army

Arriving at Schofield, I approached the sentry at the main gate, and advised that I wished to see the recruiting officer. The sentry in turn picked up his telephone, gave an extension to the operator, delivered his message, and hung up. Not long later, perhaps fifteen minutes, a driver in an Army jeep showed up, called my name, and indicated that he would take me into the base.

The Army Recruiting Officer had additional duties which took most of his time: serving as the Post Quartermaster. I was shown into his office and offered a seat. The major silently "looked" his question at me, "What are doing here?" I responded, "Major, I would like to join the Army." He stared at me as though he was seeing the dumbest person in the world. Then he said, "Son, raise your right hand."

Formalities now over, social amenities began. I explained that I was a welder at Pearl Harbor, and had worked continuously sixteen hours a day, seven days a week from December 7th until today, June 6th. I was getting tired, and felt that I would much prefer serving my country in uniform, with a weapon, and as part of a military team, rather than remaining on at Pearl Harbor.

Although eager to enlist on the spot, I learned that I would have to take an Army physical and a written test called the "Army General Classification Test." Then I would have to wait a few days for the results. When all was complete, and if I still wished, I could then face the flag, give my oath, sign my name, and join that massive fraternity known as the U.S. Army. Giving my assent, arrangements were made for me to report to the base hospital first-thing next morning to begin step one of my entry into the service. In the meantime, I was escorted to a second floor of one of the massive, multi-storied, concrete barracks and given a bunk.

The barracks were empty, and had been so since the first day of the war. All Army units were in the field, scattered throughout the island. I was shown the mess hall; the huge washrooms and shower facilities; the entertainment room with ping-pong tables, billiard tables, and radio sets; and the reading rooms. I was told to make myself at home.

It would be up to me to get to the mess hall during their hours of operation, make my appointments on time, and entertain myself as I chose, with one restriction: I was not to leave Schofield! There I was – not even a second handkerchief, let alone a change of clothing, a razor, or a toothbrush. I did make it to the Post Exchange, where I purchased razor, toothbrush, soap, and towel. People might have wondered silently about the young civilian eating at the military mess hall, making purchases at the Post Exchange, or walking about at will over the vast open areas of the Post, but no one ever questioned my business or my right to be there.


## Physical: Monday June 1st

Monday morning, I reported early at the Post hospital. It was largely deserted except for staff. I was expected, and was shown to the hospital laboratory for the taking of a blood specimen and chest x-rays. The dental clinic checked my teeth, and a record of them was made for posterity showing which, if any, the Army would be responsible for. (At that time, I had responsibility for them all!) An Army doctor took my temperature, measured my blood pressure and pulse, checked eyes, ears, and throat, had me "turn-your-head-and-cough" to check for hernia, and looked at my feet for soundness and walking capability. The doctor, in general, seemed satisfied with what was found in comparison with Army standards of acceptability. It would be a week before all results were in and I would be notified by the recruiting officer.

To pass the time, I would walk about the Post until I was tired, read in the barrack library until bored, and set up a pool table and run through the pool balls in the recreation area – which was empty, save for myself. At the mess hall, I would take a tray through the serving line and receive anything that I requested, take it to an empty table, and eat alone in a nearly empty, huge, sparkling-clean mess hall. By the time taps was sounded in the evening, I was tired enough to seek my Army cot in the otherwise deserted, huge, open squad-room and lose myself in sleep – to be awakened next morning by the Post bugler sounding reveille. After the concentrated, lengthy demands on my time and labor at the Navy Yard, the contrast of Schofield was unbelievable!

## Army General Classification Test: Tuesday June 2nd

Tuesday, I reported to personnel for the administering of the Army General Classification Test, intended to establish the parameters, capabilities, and limitations of the individual being tested. I forget the details, but it took half a day to complete and return to the person conducting the test. I was told that my score would be made a part of my permanent record and would accompany me throughout my Army career. That being the case, however, I might never learn how I had done or what it had told the Army about me.

I showered every night and morning, and shaved daily. I washed my socks and underclothing each evening, which then dried overnight for next day's use; but my slacks and shirt never got a change or freshening. During these days, there was no "people-contact," no acquaintance to make, no one to visit with. Even the Post chapel, although always open, was always deserted – and not particularly inviting. The barrack radio was welcome and the incoming voices comforting.

# Oath of Allegiance & Enlistment: Thursday June 4th

Thursday morning, a personnel clerk found me in the barrack and told me that the quartermaster officer would see me anytime after breakfast. "Do you know where he is located?" Receiving my affirmative, he departed to wherever his business took him. After showering, shaving, combing my hair, and breakfasting, I made my way across the Post to the Quartermaster area and presented myself at the Post Quartermaster's Office. "He is busy," I was told, "but is expecting you and will see you shortly. Just make yourself at home."

I have no recollection of how long I waited before being shown into the quartermaster's office. The quartermaster, an Army major in rank, rose to meet me, expressed his welcome, and extended his hand. "Have a seat," he told me, then seated himself and took a stack of papers to the center of his desk. He looked through them before raising his head once more. "Well, Drew," he said, "everything seems to be in order. Your physical results are good, your general health is excellent, the lab results are all in proper range, and..." He looked again at the last paper before him a second and third time. "And," he continued, "…your Army General Classification Test results are not bad – not bad at all. In fact, they are quite good – quite good indeed!"

"This," he said, sharing a paper with me, "...this is your Army enlistment paper." We read it over together. It indicated that I was enlisting in the Army of the United States for the period of time involved in hostilities. I read it and signed. Next, I was asked to stand and face the flag. Repeating after him, I gave my Oath of Allegiance to the Army and the United States of America. The major again invited me to sit, came over, and extended his hand. "Welcome into the Army, Drew. You are now a soldier. Do you have five dollars?"

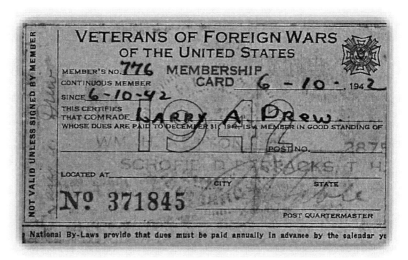

Figure 19. An immediate member of Veterans of Foreign Wars!

Puzzled, I did, and passed the bill across. Drawing a paper from his desk, the major filled it out, signed his name in two or three places, tore a portion off the page, and handed this to me. "You are now a member of the Veterans of Foreign Wars," said he. "I don't know of another person who gained membership on his very-first day in the Army. And, by the way, here is your VFW Medal which goes with membership. Congratulations." He passed it across. "This is not a part of your military dress, so just put it in your locker for now.

"You have been assigned to the Army 25th Division which is now scattered all over the island. Specifically, you will be in Headquarters Battery, 25th Division. The battery mail orderly will be here tomorrow. When he leaves the Post, he will take you with him to your new unit. The rest of the day is yours to use however you wish. Good luck." He shook my hand again, and escorted me out of his office.

# First Day with the 25th Division:
# Friday June 5th

Friday, I was seated in the mess hall, alone as usual, and having lunch. A soldier carrying his lunch tray came over and sat down across from me: "The first sergeant told me to stop before leaving the Post and pick up the new man for the battery. You must be Drew, 'cause you're the only one here. How come you're out of uniform? You look like you just got picked up by the MPs as a deserter, but then you would be in the stockade, wouldn't you? My name is Walter O'Berry. I'm the mail orderly for the battery. It's good duty." Thus it was that I met Corporal Walter O'Berry, mid-sized, early twenties, from the beef-cattle region of Florida. Up until then, I never knew that there was a large, open cattle-range in central Florida; but there were a lot of things that I didn't know.

O'Berry and I visited like old friends as we ate lunch. No one had told him that the new man was fresh into the Army the day before, but nothing really seemed to surprise him. After lunch, we drove to the Army Post Office. He disappeared inside for some time and reappeared with several, partially-full mail sacks which he loaded into the rear seat of the command car he was driving.

"Next stop," said he, "is the Personnel Office to pick up your jacket."

I gathered that the term "jacket" meant one's Army personnel folder. Again, Corporal O'Berry disappeared and reappeared shortly with a large, brown, manila envelope under his arm. This he tossed on the seat between us, started his vehicle – and together we drove off. The sentry at the main gate waved us through without stopping. I noticed that O'Berry – without changing his forward vision – was looking at me out of the side of his eye. It gave me a funny feeling. He hummed to himself as he drove, made short statements, and finally said, "You just took your AGC test, didn't you?

"Maybe so," I responded. "But to tell you the truth, I don't know what the 'AGC' test means."

"Oh, yeah," he responded. "It's our term for 'Army General Classification' test. They give it to you to figure out where to put you, so you'll do the least harm or the most good. How did you do on it?"

"Well," I replied, "the Major said that I did all right on it; that's all that I know."

O'Berry drove on, thumping the steering wheel now and then, and humming to himself. Finally he said, "Well, it's all over personnel back there, and word travels fast in the Army…and will probably beat us back to base. The word is, that you made the highest score ever-recorded in the whole 25th Division! Do you have any idea what that means?"

"I don't," I replied.

"Well," O'Berry sucked on his teeth. "…Just as well for you. No one is ever going to tell you what your AGC test score is, but lots of people in the right places are going to know, and they will all be looking at you to see what kind of person you are. You know how that is, I'm sure!"

O'Berry was a nice guy. He told me lots of things about the battery and about himself as we drove along. Pearl Harbor came into view, and the small town of Aiea. At Aiea, we made a left turn and began driving for the inland mountains. As we climbed in altitude, we began to see pine trees and then a pine forest. At the top of the ridge was a gate, before which sat a steel-helmeted soldier behind a fifty-caliber machine gun. "This is it, Drew," O'Berry told me. "We're home now."

The soldier rose, waved to O'Berry, opened the gate for him, and closed it again as soon as the vehicle had cleared the entrance. Presently, along each side of the dirt road, could be seen six-man paramble tents and a mess fly-canopy with Army field-ranges set up and operating. There were picnic-type tables with benches on each side, providing "sit-down-to-eat" facilities for the men. Nearby was a small, screened tent obviously serving as mess tent for the officers of the battery. A few men were in sight. On up the road and around a bend, we came to another set of two tents. O'Berry pulled his vehicle to a halt in front of one, parked, and turned the vehicle off. "This is Headquarter's tent," said he. "Come with me, and I'll introduce you to the first sergeant and to the battery clerk."

Inside, I met Staff Sergeant Hayes, the battery clerk: a regular-Army man in his early thirties, scholarly looking. Behind him, I met First Sergeant Lloyd Turner: mid-sized, sturdy, mid-to-late thirties, obviously a regular-Army man. Turner grinned and shook my hand. "Welcome to the Army, Drew," he said, looking me up and down. "Do you have any gear with you?"

"No gear," I replied. "I come just as you see me."

Obviously, Turner liked that. "Well," he said, "we'll do something about that real soon. Can't have you going around the battery looking like that, or – God knows what some of the other men might decide to do."

60

Turner took my personnel jacket, which Sergeant Hayes had been looking at. He leafed through the pages. Now and then, he made a sound to himself. Once he looked at a single page, and returned his attention to it two-or-three more times. O'Berry looked at me – gave a wink and a grin. "See, I told you," was his silent communication. Turner returned my jacket to Sergeant Hayes, who opened a file drawer, placed the folder inside, and closed the file. "Come with me, Drew," Turner spoke again. "We'll go over to the supply tent and see what our supply sergeant can do with you."

We moved from headquarters tent to the large supply tent next door. Here I met Technical Sergeant Pate: mid-forties, slender, balding, and obviously very capable. Pate was assisted by Supply Corporal Joe Clark: mid-twenties, slim, nice-looking, and the widest grin you could ever imagine. "This is our newest recruit," Turner said as he introduced me. "Let's see if you can't get him into some decent clothing, shall we?"

Pate looked me up-and-down and began giving sizes and quantities to Corporal Clark, who wrote them down on a new-issue card bearing my name and rank: "Drew, Larry A. Private Army Serial Number (ASN) 10 100 324." These numbers told everyone that I had entered the Army overseas, and that I was the 324th person ever to do so.

Army clothing is generally colored "OD," short for "olive drab." In the tropics, however, it is colored "suntan." I don't recall the quantities each of issue, but it was sufficient to enable one to always have a clean uniform, plus uniforms en route to-and-from the laundry. Laundry was collected once weekly and hauled to the Army laundry facility at Schofield for processing and return. The cost for this service was relatively inexpensive, and was taken directly from one's monthly pay before one received the remaining balance. I received socks: cotton; socks: wool; shoes: each, two pair; underwear: OD; slacks: suntan and shirts: suntan; overseas work uniforms: regulation blue; hat:

work, cotton, soft-brim, blue; blankets: wool, OD, each, two; mattress-cover: white, each, two; gas-mask: each, one; web-belt: complete, including canteen and aid-kit; rifle: each, Springfield bolt-action, each, one; ammunition: caliber 30, each, one bandoleer of 100 rounds. During all of this, Sergeant Pate never asked me for a single item of information, and yet his announced-sizes fit perfectly!

Before leaving the supply tent, I was relieved of all the clothing which I had arrived in, and I exited the supply tent dressed like every other man in the battery. After all, I was a soldier. My cotton barracks-bag now full of new Army-issue clothing and blankets, Sergeant Hayes escorted me to my new, temporary home: a six-man paramble tent having a vacant, canvas cot available for me. The other tent occupants were men newly-arrived from the Army "Repl Depl" (short for "Replacement Depot"). They were all draftees who had received basic training in the U.S., and then shipped overseas to the Army Replacement Depot for assignment to various units as needed. Some of the men were in their mid-twenties, a few in their thirties.

For normal battery duty, the dress was suntan and always included the "gas-mask-with-steel helmet" loosely hung over the front. Even when free "on pass," the gas-mask and steel helmet were part of the uniform. The blue "fatigue" uniform was worn on work details such as kitchen police (KP), or by the mechanics at the motor section. The wire section wore blue or suntan, according to what they were doing. The drivers from the transportation motor section always wore suntan.

At dinner my first night with the battery, Sergeant Hayes took me over to the noncom table and introduced me to Sergeant Barnes, a soft-spoken Texan. Sergeant Barnes, he told me, was in charge of the "Wire Section." I had been assigned to him for duty, beginning next day. Our battery, I learned, was a support battery for Headquarters Division Artillery. Its sections consisted of mess, motor, radio communication, wire and telephone communication, meteorology (weather), survey, and supply.

# The Wire Section

In the Wire Section, I quickly learned the use of climbing-irons to scale trees or telephone poles; how to unreel or recover telephone wire from the rear of a moving vehicle; how to set up field telephones and switchboards, etc. It was our job to string and maintain all wire between Artillery Headquarters and Headquarters of each of the four battalions of artillery. We also manned the Division Artillery Headquarters switchboard on an around-the-clock schedule.

# Basic Training: All in a Day

One day, I spent cleaning my rifle: It had been issued to me still encased in the wax-like grease, "cosmoline," applied to preserve it at the end of WWI! This task took most of the day. Next day, Sergeant Barnes took me to the bottom of a nearby, isolated canyon, set up a target, and showed me how to shoot. He demonstrated how to "zero in" the sights to ensure that what I looked at would also be what I hit. He left me there to shoot at my own pace – a full bandoleer consisting of 100 rounds of ammunition. This done, I was to find my way back to the battery. With practice, I found how to hold my rifle to the shoulder and get the least recoil. That old rifle, however, was really powerful and had plenty of kick. My shoulder was swollen and sore for days afterward. This one, single day constituted my entire period of basic training, compared to the three months which all the others had received.

# Second Day with the Battery:
# "Loaning to Buddies"

On my second day with the battery, one of the men approached me in chow line and hesitantly asked if I could loan him twenty dollars "until payday." Without hesitation, I could and did. Then again, hesitantly, he asked how much interest I was going to charge, to which I replied: "Hell, I don't charge interest to a buddy!" This was hard for him to accept; so he checked again, and then asked with still more hesitation: "Well then, could you maybe let me have another twenty?" Again, I could and did.

Good news travels fast, and I have no idea how many men found me in the chow line and asked for loans! I never kept a notebook with names or amounts; but always after payday, each in turn sought me out and repaid in full! Some might ask for a loan as soon as they had paid, but they always paid first. I had been sending nearly all of my Pearl Harbor wages back to Ohio in care of my mother, but still had my last paycheck in hand. Thus – to the men of my battery – I was seen as the rich, ex-defense worker who had money to lend and who did not charge interest to his buddies.

## Switchboard Duty

I wasn't in the wire section very long before being assigned to switchboard duty at Division Headquarters. I would be on night shift, because it normally had lighter switchboard-activity and they felt that the new man could handle that safely by himself. Before being left on my own, however, I sat with a daytime operator for a couple of days, observing his procedure. Then, under his supervision, I would take a turn myself. There was a certain switchboard politeness to learn and observe: care was to be exercised to make certain that when ringing the requested party, the operator never rang in the ear of the requesting party. People had been known to become angry and even abusive should the operator inadvertently ring in one's ear! When my tutor, Corporal Lowe, deemed me acceptable, I was moved to night shift on my own. My performance must have been acceptable and uncriticized, because I remained there until it came my turn at "KP" duty.

## Kitchen Police Duty: "KP"

KP duty was assigned on a rotating-roster basis and was "pulled" by all privates and privates first class – which was most of the battery. On this duty, we reported early to the mess sergeant and remained late, until all was scrubbed to his satisfaction. We then closed down for the night. Duty varied from peeling potatoes to going as labor with the ration truck when it went to Schofield for rations. There was lots of dishwashing in hot, soapy water: known as "pearl diving" in the Army. You might even assist a cook on the serving line should they need assistance. KP wasn't bad duty because Sergeant McKee always had a few perks for his KPs – like extra rations of the best food, extra dessert, and even snacks not available to anyone else.

My week of KP over, I fell in with the rest of the battery for Saturday morning inspection, after which a one-day pass could be had for the asking. When Lt. Wainwright, the battery exec, came to me, he looked me over closely and frowned at what he saw. "Why are you standing inspection unshaved?" he asked.

"Sir," I responded, "I am just finishing my week's KP and planned to go to town on pass. I was planning to shave just before leaving."

"Not good enough soldier," he replied. "When you stand inspection, you stand ready for duty, and obviously you're not. First Sergeant," Lt. Wainwright continued, "put this man down for an extra week of KP to reinforce his memory." It was right then that I decided to make corporal as soon as I could, because corporals and above never pulled KP!

# An Opening in the Survey Section: Transfer Requested

Switchboard operator duty was considered very desirable because that was all one had to do. Off-hours were generally one's own. After a few weeks, however, it became more and more boring to me; and when Staff Sergeant Ashcroft, head of Survey Section, applied for the Flying Cadets and was accepted, I saw an opportunity. Approaching the first sergeant, I told him that if possible, I would like to be considered for assignment to the survey section. Turner asked if I was unhappy with my assignment and I replied that I was not, but felt that I could be valuable in survey. In response, Turner told me that I would have to discuss it with the battery commander. Thus, the next day I made myself crisp and shining, and presented myself at the orderly tent.

Enlisted men generally stayed the hell away from officers because they felt uncomfortable and out of place in their presence. Also, enlisted men could only speak directly to an officer if they had the first sergeant's permission to do so. Sergeant Turner protected the officers as much as possible from such invasions of their time. Fortunately, I had learned my drill well at Ohio State during my two years of Reserve Officer Training Corps (ROTC). I knocked at the battery commander's door and waited until I received his "come in." Then I marched in, removed my hat, and stood at attention. The captain was busy with papers requiring his attention, but in all reality was surely looking me over. I stood before him, straight and head high, looking forward. He looked up. This was my signal that I now had his attention. I snapped a salute and held it. "Sir," I stated firmly, "Private Drew had the First Sergeant's permission to speak to the Battery Commander."

Captain Misha Kadick, probably eight years my senior, returned my salute. "At ease, Drew," he said. "You're the new man in the battery, aren't you? Is everything going alright for you? Have you any complaints?"

"Sir," I replied, "everything is just fine. I like the Army, I like the battery, and I like the duty just fine." Captain Kadick was obviously pleased to hear this. Too often it was gripes or fights he heard of – those which the first sergeant couldn't handle.

"Well then," he said, "what brings you here?"

"Sir," I spoke again, "with Sergeant Ashcroft leaving for the Flying Cadets, it occurs to me that there may be a vacancy in the Survey Section. If there is, I would surely like to be considered. I have a couple years of college at Ohio State University, and believe that I could contribute. I believe that the work would be more demanding also."

Captain Kadick listened. "I've seen your jacket," he said, "and although there isn't much in it, it looks good. Let me take a day or two to look into it, and I'll get back to you." Looking squarely at me again, he asked, "Is there anything else?"

"No Sir," I replied, "and I wish to thank the Captain for his time." I stood at attention, saluted, and held it.

"You're welcome, Drew," the Captain replied, returning my salute. "Dismissed!"

I turned smartly and departed from his office. Outside, Sergeant Hayes was waiting. "How did it go, Drew?" he asked.

"All right, as best I could tell," I answered. "Thank the First Sergeant for permission to see the Captain." I went back to my tent and changed uniform for my next job.

## Southern Officers the Rule

I found it very interesting that most of the regular-Army men of the battery were Southerners and even more interesting that all of the noncommissioned officers (NCOs) were Southerners! Not a single Yankee noncom or officer in the entire battery. Both Captain Kadick, Battery Commander, and Lt. Wainwright, Battery Executive Officer, were graduates of VMI (Virginia Military Institute) known as the "West Point of the South." The bulk of battery supervision was accomplished by Lt. Wainwright (nephew of General Wainwright of Bataan). Captain Kadick spent most of his time at Division Artillery Headquarters where he had additional duties on the staff of Division Artillery Commander, Brigadier General Stanley Reinhart. When we did see Captain Kadick, addressing the battery in formation or walking through on inspection, he was always closely followed at heel by his big, male, German shepherd dog: "Lightning," by name. In the Captain's office, Lightning would lie, half-attentively with one eye open, at his master's feet. Now and again, the captain's pretty, young wife would show up at the battery for lunch at the officers' mess tent.

On those days, Lightning would be seen as her close, and very attentive, escort.

## Request Granted:
## Assigned to Survey

Sergeant Ashcroft departed the battery a few days later. Shortly afterward, Sergeant Barnes told me that I was to be moved from the tent of the wire section to residence with the men of the survey section. Anxiously it seemed, he asked if I had been unhappy about my work in his section, or about my treatment or duty assignment as switchboard operator. I assured Sergeant Barnes that I felt good about all that had happened to me since my arrival in the battery. I especially appreciated his personal time and attention, and the tutoring which I had received from him. I liked the wire section and the duty, but felt that the survey work was more challenging, and I liked the opportunity to learn. This seemed to satisfy Sergeant Barnes and we always remained on the best of terms.

The Survey Section at this time consisted of five men: Corporal Darrel Gordon, now in charge; Private First Class Michael Ready; Private First Class John Joseph Pershing Walsh; Private Lenzie Russell; and now myself. The section had two surveyor transits, stadia rods with small, red & white bull's-eye on top, and measuring chains. The job was to provide survey coverage for the division, make maps for use in fire-direction for the artillery, and locate targets of opportunity for artillery concentration-fire. The section went into the field every day: throughout the mountains, across pineapple fields, around sugarcane fields. We surveyed wherever the artillery needed to know the exact location of battalions and firing batteries, and produced maps showing the location of potential targets in relation to the batteries. It was good duty.

Corporal Gordon was one year my senior and regular-Army. He was always direct in letting others know what he thought:

"It's absolutely unheard of for the newest man in the battery to be assigned to Survey," were his first words to me. "Why, there are men here who have been dying for the opportunity for over a year. With our section so small, there is hardly ever a chance for them. You must have some kind of suction with the brass or the officers! Hell, they didn't even ask me, or give me a chance to say who I might have recommended...Sergeant Turner just told me that you were my new man. I should really resent your being assigned to me, but you seem to be a decent sort... 'not pushy, not a pain in the ass,' according to Sergeant Barnes. The men all seem to like you well enough. So...welcome to the Survey Section." He extended his hand. "By the way, do you know anything about logarithms, seven-place tables, trigonometry, and such? If not, you're gonna have one hell of a time! And," he added, "what about 'aiming circle' work? Do you know anything about that?"

I told him that I could find my way through log tables and knew the difference between sines, cosines, tangents, cotangents, secants, and cosecants. I knew what each measured and how to figure the others. I also told him that I knew my way around the French artillery aiming-circle, which even now was the standard aiming-instrument for our artillery pieces.

Gordon scratched his head and grinned. "Well, if all that is in your jacket," he said, "I guess I can see why they picked you for the job. Hell, I wouldn't have had a clue, except for the way you came into the battery so unexpectedly. I guess I shouldn't have been surprised. You obviously have work experience and education going for you."

# Fatigue Duty and Camp Routine

Most of the men available for "fatigue duty," – an Army word for "labor parties" – were now spending most of their time turning the dirt roads into gravel-surfaced roads. The also erected tarpaper-covered plywood shacks to replace the canvas tents. This would turn our part of the pine forest into a more permanent camp. As they progressed, each section in turn folded its tent and turned it back to battery supply. A shack was about eight feet by ten feet in floor space, and had room for six men sleeping in double bunks. The floor was on pilings and was perhaps a foot or so above ground level. Needless to say, the shacks were much warmer than the tents and quite welcome.

Battery duty was now a routine. First came reveille, followed by the entire battery forming in the road in front of the headquarters tent for roll call and any special words from the battery commander. Breakfast followed roll call, and then each section organized and went their individual way. The survey crew always loaded into a weapons carrier and set off to some part of the island where we continued to shoot horizontal and vertical angles, and to determine the distances between each station which had been occupied by the transit. Careful and precise field-notes were made, to be used later in mathematical calculations. All of this came together in the form of precise maps, which were invaluable in any artillery problem.

# The Chief

If you happened to see the movie "From Here to Eternity," you may remember the Territorial Boxing Champ. It just so happened that he actually existed, and was a member of our battery. He was a full-blooded Cherokee from Oklahoma, named Woodie Chandler, and nicknamed "Chief." The Chief was an easy-going person – until, that is, he got drunk. Then, it was "look out!" For some reason, however – and I have no idea why – the Chief had taken a liking to me and trusted me. Thus it was, that whenever it was "look-out-for-the-Chief!" time, someone always came for me. I seemed to be known to the entire battery as "the Kid." Our drunken Chief would flatten almost anyone when in this condition, but would let me take charge of him with no resistance. I would show up, get him over to our survey shack, and settle him down on my bunk until he had slept off his binge. Upon awakening to his usual self, he would happily shower and return to his own shack.

One rainy night, Chief"s shack roof developed a leak, which the drunken Chief decided to fix. Instead of fixing it, however, Chief fell off the roof and broke his back. In the Army of this time, a soldier recorded "good-time" and "bad-time." "Good-time" was that which happened "in line of duty." "Bad-time" was that which happened "not in line of duty." "Bad-time" was added on to the end of one's enlistment, and had to be worked off. People came silently to the rescue of the Chief: He was put on a stretcher and taken into shelter, where he was kept while being sobered up and cleaned up. Then, an ambulance from the motor pool was brought up to take him to the hospital under medical escort. Chief was placed in a body cast from his hips to his neck. When he could get a pass from Schofield, he would come and visit us. I forget the official story about how he was hurt, but it was entered as "line of duty." I imagine that even our first sergeant was in on taking care of Chief, but am equally certain that the officers never had a clue about what had happened. He never returned to the battery after being released from the hospital.

Figure 20. Training in Hawaii. From left: Larry Drew with fellow infantrymen of the 25<sup>th</sup> Division. (Personal Photo)

## Training for Full Scale Maneuvers

In late summer, we learned that the division was about to engage in full-scale maneuvers. "Army problems" were being run all over the island – the worst being those which took us around the cane fields. These were heavily irrigated and unbelievably full of mosquitoes. There was no way to protect oneself from these awful insects, and sleeping was worst of all. Even under mosquito nets, they could turn a piece of you into raw flesh overnight. We hiked all over the mountains using the pack-trails of mule artillery. We took these narrow paths down to the sea and back up into the clouds again: all with full backpacks, weapons, and steel helmets. It was interesting how rapidly one developed really rugged muscles under this routine.

Taken out to sea equipped with full pack, weapon, and life jacket, we were put overboard a mile or so offshore to make our way to land as best we could. All ships use "cargo nets," which are hooked to a ship's winches to load and off-load cargo. A cargo net is about 40 feet square. It looks like a giant window screen with the mesh one foot each way – instead of a fraction of an inch each way. The mesh is made up of heavy rope about an inch in diameter. The net is very, very strong.

For off-loading troops where there are no piers, cargo nets are secured by one side to the ship's deck, with the remaining net allowed to hang overboard. Men will climb over the railing, grasp the cargo net firmly, place their feet onto the horizontal portion of the mesh, and proceed to climb down into the small boats waiting below. The net can hold as many men as are able to be on it at any one time. The sway and lurch of the ship's motion add to the challenge; but strong men can handle the procedure and maneuver safely into the awaiting boats. We suffered no casualties during the cargo net off-loading; however, the heavy pack, rifle, and life jacket chafed our shoulders, armpits, chests, and waists. Salt water managed to splash into and rub these tender areas of skin during the trip from ship to shore; it aggravated the chafed spots, making one pretty sore.

Figure 21. Amphibious drills and intense training exercises in preparation for the coming offensive action in the Pacific. US Army photo reprinted from *The 25th Division and World War 2* (p 18), Cpt. Robert F. Karolevitz, ed., 1946, Army and Navy Publishing Co.

Figures 22 and 23. Hawaii was the site of intensive training, numerous amphibious drills, and long hours of preparation for the coming offensive action in the Pacific. US Army photos reprinted from *The 25th Division and World War 2* (p 18), Cpt. Robert F. Karolevitz, ed., 1946, Army and Navy Publishing Company.

# A Close Brush with the System

One of the men disappeared from the battery one day with never a word. Michael was older, perhaps thirty-five. He was quiet, soft-spoken, and thoughtful, a well-educated man and a sculptor. The rest of the battery were being given physical exams, apparently being checked out for fitness to continue the very arduous training exercises. A couple of weeks later, Michael reappeared at the battery: He had been in the Schofield Mental Ward. How this came about, I have no idea. Michael talked about his experience to the six or seven of us who had been close to him. He had been very careful of his actions and in how he expressed himself in order to make the best impression possible as to his normalcy and coping skills. He had been in great fear of being retained in the mental ward. Obviously, he had been successful in convincing the medical staff of his normalcy.

# Who Stayed and Who Would Go

Following the physical exams, First Sergeant Turner was moved from the battery with no explanation. Technical Sergeant Pate of Supply was removed from the battery the same day also. Staff Sergeant Granger turned himself in at sick call with a "bad-time" ailment, and was gone. "Bad-time" meant that he would automatically be reduced in rank from staff sergeant to private. Our heavy-weight boxing champ, Woodie Chandler, was gone with the others. There were a lot of rumors about what was going on, but no one really seemed to have an accurate fix on it.

# Chuck Babcock, Orderly –
# A Happy Solution

Chuck Babcock stayed with us. He may have been twenty years old. On the day after he graduated from high school, his father took him to see the Army recruiter; and from this, Chuck became a soldier. He was nice-looking, slim, stood straight and tall, and wanted everyone to like him – as we did. We even sympathized with his mental slowness. There was not a job in any section which fit Babcock, so they finally made him a "PLO" (permanent latrine orderly). Babcock fell to his work with enthusiasm and always had the latrines sparkling. Then the brass learned that they could not assign any one man to permanent latrine duty. Babcock was out of a job, until next they made him a permanent KP – temporarily also, and for the same reason. After this, he became orderly for the battery officers' mess. In his suntan trousers and white mess-jacket, Babcock looked great; and this was the job of which he was most proud. He always stood straight and tall in the mess tent, and looked after the officers' every need at breakfast, lunch, dinner, snacks, or coffee, whenever or wherever asked. He remained on this assignment – a happy solution.

# Shipping Out

Then one day, acting Supply Sergeant Joe Clark had a footlocker issued to each of the battery. On the cover, we each stenciled our name and home address, and were instructed to fill it with all non-issue possessions. When turned in next day, they would each begin their way homeward. *NOW WE LEARNED FROM THE BATTERY COMMANDER HIMSELF THAT WE WERE SHIPPING OUT,* and in a matter of days! When the day came for us to break camp, we each had a field pack with clothing, two wool blankets, a "shelter-half" (pup tent) and stakes, entrenching tool, weapon, ammunition, web belt complete with canteen and first-aid pouch, and steel helmet. Gas masks were turned in.

We loaded on board large, six-wheel-drive Army trucks by section; and when camp was struck, rode down the mountain out of our pine forest and down through the town of Aiea. There, we turned and drove past Pearl Harbor, Boys Town, and Hickam Field, past the cane fields, and into Honolulu. Here, we pulled alongside of a huge, grey, ocean-going ship at pierside next to the Aloha Tower. We all dismounted the trucks and – forming as a battery – remained in formation: allowed to "stand at ease" and talk, but not to smoke.

When it came our turn to board, we moved in single file past the first sergeant and battery clerk, who each held a roster of the names of all men in our battery. As we filed past, we each stated name, rank, and scrial number. The battery clerk and first sergeant made facial recognition, verifying that each man was indeed whom he stated to be. A check mark was made after the name, and the person then mounted the gangway to move on board.

A Navy bosun took charge of our battery column, and led the way across deck into an open, watertight door which gave way to a steel ladder leading below decks. Our area was the second deck below the main deck, and consisted of a large cargo-hold which had been fitted to provide bunk space for troops. Each aisle of bunks was stacked six or eight bunks high on either side. Each bunk was long enough for a man to lie down full-length, plus room at the foot for a full field-pack. A person could sit on his bunk also, but the next-higher bunk would hit him a bit below the shoulders, creating a most uncomfortable crouching position. We were told to settle into our bunks and to remain there until told otherwise.

# Chapter 5.
# On Board the *Noordam* – Destination Unknown
## November 25, 1942

Figure 24. *M.V. Noordam* (A Dutch passenger cargo ship) shown at San Francisco, California about 1943 as a troopship. US Navy Photo NH 89832

## Our New Accommodations

It was hot, and humid, and stuffy in our below-decks compartment. Change of air was provided by way of cloth tubes about three feet across, which extended from above deck down into each hold. Every tube had its own motorized fan to move the air. The contraption was better than nothing and, obviously, the happy solution of some mechanical engineer.

The troops of the battery remained in place along with the chief of each section. The battery NCO brass moved around the aisles allotted to our unit, talking to the men, listening to them, and exchanging information. There were many rumors, of course. The best one, a product of the old-timers, was this: "We were a regular-Army division. We had already been overseas more than three years. Our greatest value to the war would be to train the Army now being built up by the draft. We would soon be returned Stateside. There, the division would be broken up into smaller cadre units, each to be the training nucleus of a new and larger unit."

Finally, the loading of troops was completed, and we were allowed to leave our barrack-area in the hold of the ship and move about. Below decks, there were some hold-areas open to all personnel. These included huge, food-preparation and eating areas; large saltwater-shower facilities; large toilet-facilities; and a ship service-area where goods such as snacks, tobacco, soap, razors, writing paper, and envelopes were sold. It would be open for business as soon as we were out to sea.

Above deck, restricted areas were roped-off, and roped paths directed movement of personnel. Our ship was the Motor Vessel *Noordam*, a very new ship of the Holland American Steamship Company, now on lease to the U.S. Government. Officers were Dutch and the crew mostly Polish, with a small group of men native to Dutch Indonesia. The Poles spoke only their native language and the native crew spoke Dutch. Fortunately, several of our battery were first- or second-generation Americans of Polish ancestry who spoke Polish fluently, and we began to learn their language. The ship's mascot was a small fox-terrier who had full run of the ship. Interestingly, he only responded to spoken Polish!

That afternoon, as a unit 200-strong, we made our way into the dining-hold, made a single file, and went through the mess line. Each man used his field mess-kit and canteen cup. Afterward, each was responsible for properly cleaning his own gear. This helped lessen the load on the hard-worked kitchen staff. Since every battery or company on board had their own mess section, the unit mess sections were put to work on a roster basis in the dining-holds. Mess Sergeant McKee always stood at the head of the wash-up line, making certain that each man gave proper attention to washing and drying his mess equipment. It was as though McKee personally owned every mess kit in the battery, and intended to make sure that his equipment was properly cared for – and indeed it was!

# Promotion to Corporal

That first day aboard ship, Sergeant Gordon, Chief of the Survey Section, sought me out and took me aside: "Drew," he began, "the brass told me that they have promoted you to corporal. Now I want you to know that it wasn't my idea. Hell, they didn't even ask me who I would want to be promoted. They just told me! Lenzie Russell would have been my man, had they asked!" Lenzie was ten years my senior, a Southerner from Huntsville, Alabama, and my best buddy. I had long been aware that every noncom in the battery was a Southerner – up to now, that is. "I should have known," Gordon continued. "At our regular, weekly noncom meetings with the battery commander, he always would ask me how the new man was doing. I would always reply that you were doing just great, and were a welcome addition to the section. He never asked me about any of the other men, just about my new man. I guess, in a way, I am personally responsible for your being promoted. Well then," he continued, "I have this to give you: it is your warrant promoting you to corporal. Hell, you never even made it to private first class and now you're corporal! That's the new Army for you." Gordon passed the paper over to me, signed by the battery commander, and certifying that I was now Corporal Drew, U.S. Army. Gordon extended his hand to shake mine. "Welcome to the Battery NCO Club," he said. "One thing that goes with it is that you never have to pull KP duty – ever again."

# Ship Life on the Way to…?

It was still daylight above decks, and we could see that the three ships in our group were all being loaded. My guess was that as many as 10,000 men were being processed on board the three vessels. We learned that the rest of the division would be following about a week after our departure.

Sometime during the quiet of that first night, as I lay in my bunk, I could feel a free movement telling me that *Noordam* had left the pier and was in motion. After a time, one could hear the sound of water slapping the outer side of the ship's steel hull. Later still, a slight, rolling motion could be detected – and then an up-and-down motion as the ship would mount a wave and slide down its other side. Eventually we were getting a side-to-side rolling action and an up-and-down action at the same time. This became monotonous and disconcerting, and soon provided an introduction to seasickness!

I went above deck and walked about – enjoying the fresh air and quietness. The deck was largely deserted. Our ship was underway with no visible light anywhere: in total blackout. No other ships were visible. Returning below deck, I had to pass through a double blackout-curtain, designed to prevent any interior light from being visible outside. Inside at night, only dim, blue lights were used to provide adequate lighting for moving about. They lit up the shower, toilet, and mess spaces. It was mildly hot below deck, and notably quiet with so many men bedded down in their narrow bunks. I turned in and slept surprisingly well.

No bugle sounded next morning, but I was awake at the time reveille would have sounded anyhow. I was among those early in the shower and latrine: dressed and ready before the battery began to line up and move out for its turn in the breakfast-hold. Breakfast was ample and excellent: I had my choice of toast, sausage, eggs, pancakes, canned fruit – any or all. I didn't have to take it all at once, but could eat what I wished and return for duplicates or a "passed-by-first" item. They even had milk made from a reconstituted, dried product and water. It was what the Navy called their "mechanical cow" product, and it was pretty good. After breakfast, I washed my field mess-gear to Sergeant McKee's satisfaction, thanked him when he congratulated me on my being promoted, and returned to my bunk to rid myself of my mess gear until needed again at noontime.

I noticed right away that we were not headed east as many of the regulars had predicted. The sun rose behind us, and set ahead. We were obviously going westward and southward. With daylight, I could make out two other vessels some distance away, heading in the same general direction as *Noordam*. "Probably the two ships which had been loading troops alongside us," I thought. During the day, I could also observe the Morse code traffic being transmitted between ships by means of Navy signal-lights. Our ship changed direction now and then to make it harder for submarines to pick up a traffic pattern; but, in general, we steadily moved in a south-westerly direction. Australia was the only thought which came to my mind, but I did not express the thought to anyone.

Exercise came to me in the form of climbing up and down ladders, doing push-ups in the narrow aisle separating the bunk columns, doing pull-ups from the overhead pipe stanchions in the shower room, and running in place above deck in the fresh air. There was no organized physical exercise of any kind; actually, there was no room anywhere for organized exercise.

I never figured out where the officers were quartered, and don't recall seeing any officers of the battery, although there was a daily meeting of the battery commander and the section chiefs. I, like all the others, was largely left alone to pass the time, more or less, as I chose.

Many of the men on board were obviously seasick now. They stayed in their bunks much of the time, and took nourishment from snacks and soft drinks purchased from the ship's service canteen. Although my stomach was uneasy, I made it a point to never miss a meal, and am certain that it helped me avoid the real nausea so many were experiencing. In the mess hold, chow lines were noticeably shorter and took less time to clear.

Gordon had a word for everything. On seasickness, he said: "Hell, there is nothing at all weak about my stomach. At the ship's rail, I can heave my lunch as far as any man on ship." When looking for Gordon, you had only to find the nearest poker game, knowing that he would be in the middle of it.

## Invading Neptune's Realm: Crossing the Equator

Amidship on the main deck, the Navy men were rigging a swimming pool out of canvas hatch-covers. It was thirty or forty feet square and four or five feet deep. When finished, they began filling it with ocean water by making use of the ship's fire-fighting system. Oddly, after it was finished, they began tossing garbage into the pool. By next day, it was noticeably pungent.

Each day was a bit warmer than the day before: obviously because we were still going south. And then, one early afternoon, King Neptune and his Court came aboard to take over the ship! Our ship had invaded Neptune's realm, we were told, and had done so without permission. The only way to atone was to become a "shellback" and swear allegiance to Neptune. At the moment, we were all "polliwogs" and were fair-hunting for all of Neptune's following.

The first person to be tried at Neptune's Court was the "Number One Polliwog" on board: Major General J. Lawton Collins, himself! Until then, I hadn't even known that General Collins was on board our ship! Collins was unceremoniously tossed into the garbage pool along with any of his staff whom the boarding party could find. Each was scrubbed thoroughly with a rough broom, checked by the Royal Doctor and inoculated for protection against "Equator Fever." Somewhere along the line, each was presented to the Royal Baby (who was clad only in royal diaper and bonnet), to "kiss the arse" of the Royal Baby. They then professed allegiance to Neptune, "now and forever," and agreed to protect the realm of Neptune against all trespassers.

The troops of the ship received less personal attention than the brass, but were well-hosed down with saltwater fire-hoses, and dosed "medicinely." One and all received odd, and varied, and indeed individually-unique hair-carvings; gentian-violet and iodine skin-paintings; and anything else which the imaginative shellbacks could think of imposing. Those in sick bay may have been left alone, but hardly anyone else was. Having crossed the equator, still proceeding south and west, King Neptune and his Royal Court stepped overboard and disappeared back to the central part of Neptune's kingdom.

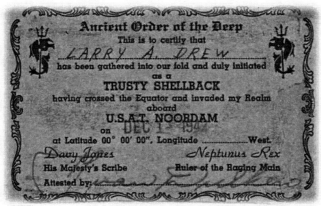

Figure 25. My certification as a "Trusty Shellback"
upon crossing the Equator

# A Good Night's Sleep on Deck

Nights were generally clear and somewhat cool. The sky was full of stars: I found the "Southern Cross," and also realized that the "North Star" no longer shown in the sky. It was still up there, but it was only visible in the Northern Hemisphere. At night too, the entire open-space of the main deck was covered by men who chose the steel deck and fresh air to the hot, stuffy holds. The ship's newspaper had a short statement about sleeping on deck. It went: "The men sleeping on deck wish you to know that they do not mind being stepped on as you move about the ship, but please do not stand on them while you try to find your bearings."

The ship's newspaper also had a daily account on the progress of the War, both in North Africa and in the Pacific. The Japs were still expanding the War with new invasions and had taken additional territories from the Dutch, British, and Australians. At the moment, their navy seemed more powerful than our depleted navy.

# Land Sighted! New Caledonia

I have no recollection of how long we were at sea with no sight of land, but finally land was recognized ahead of us, very low on the horizon. As I watched, fascinated, it ever-so-slowly grew more recognizable, rising more and more above the horizon. The jaggedness of mountains took shape. Eventually tree forms could be recognized, followed in time by the uneven outline of buildings low on the horizon. It was the island of New Caledonia, I learned: A French possession, it was now being controlled by the "Free French," and of value because of its rich deposits of chromium and nickel ore. Currently, ships came to this area of the world full with military cargo, and would return eastward filled with these valuable ores, much needed in the war effort.

Our three ships entered a quiet, lagoon-like harbor, the shore lined with tall coconut trees. Approaching a pier, each of our three ships was soon tied alongside. Section chiefs advised that we were not disembarking, but would be in port for a day or so.

Shore to ship activity began as soon as we were tied up. An endless fleet of material-handling equipment began delivering crates and large boxes alongside; and the ships' cranes began bringing them on board. Nothing went below because the spaces below deck were already full. Instead, it was all placed into tall, mountain-like stacks on the main deck, and secured in place to prevent shifting. The ships were also taking on fuel and fresh water supplies. These were delivered by large hoses about as round as a gallon bucket in diameter. Except for time off for eating or showering, I stayed above deck and watched. Even after dark, the work never stopped until completed sometime the next day.

In harbor were many US Navy ships – the first I had seen since leaving Hawaii. Someone pointed out the island's Catholic cathedral to me. I was told it had been built by prison labor. The island held a large, French prison population along with its dark-skinned Melanesian population, most of whom worked in the mines.

On the afternoon of the second day, our ship's engines again came to life. Each ship was cast off from its moorings, slowly moved away from pierside, and gradually got underway. We were obviously putting to sea again. I could see that other Navy ships were leaving at the same time as ourselves, and could recognize three or four huge battlecruisers and several destroyers moving out to take position ahead, astern, port, and starboard of our own three ships.

# General Collin's Announcement:
# Destination Guadalcanal

By the time dusk was approaching, we had been to sea for a couple of hours. Each ship had a very good public-address system used to pass orders to ship's personnel or information to all hands on board. I had become expert enough to recognize the sound of the "PA" system being turned on, and to turn and listen to whatever we were intended to hear. As dusk approached, I heard it activated. A voice began:

"This is General Collins speaking. I want to thank each of you for being such excellent passengers under these difficult conditions. I know you have heard every rumor imaginable about where we are going and what we are doing. Finally, I can tell you: Three mornings from now, about break of day, we are going ashore on the island of Guadalcanal."

The ship was in absolute silence for the longest minute – and then from every voice on board, the men spoke with a tremendous cheer! It was deafening and long. As the sound died down, I could hear similar cheering from the other two ships. Their reaction had been identical to ours!

General Collins continued: "I have arranged for Marine NCOs, fresh from Guadalcanal, to be air-transported down from the island to meet us. They are now on board each of our ships and have been assigned to small units. They will remain with us until we land, and will share their experiences with each of us. I caution you to listen well to what they will be telling you, because your knowledge may very well save your life. Effective immediately, rank insignia will be removed: whether general, corporal, private first class or in between. There will be no more saluting or addressing by rank or title; after all, everyone knows who everyone is anyhow. I want every weapon loaded; and for now, the safety put on. I want no accidental weapon-discharges; but you are cautioned to not have an unloaded weapon from now, until I personally tell you otherwise."

"Remember," General Collins cautioned, "The Jap have proven themselves to be treacherous, mean, bestial, and determined adversaries. If, when you get ashore, you see a Jap and are uncertain if he is dead or "playing possum," put another round in the man to make sure. We are not taking prisoners. We are going to give the Jap one hell of a licking."

Once again, as one, the men in the ships roared their approval. They each were expressing their desire and grim intention to war with the Jap who had bombed them at Pearl Harbor.

There had already been three, huge, naval battles in the waters around Guadalcanal. In each, the Jap had fought better than we. Ship losses were large on both sides. The enemy was bringing more and more troops ashore and fully intended to retake the island completely. High officials of the U.S. Navy were beginning to favor abandoning Guadalcanal to the enemy. General Vandergrift of the Marines was fearful that he might not be able to hold the beachhead. When this information came to the attention of President Roosevelt, he was determined to hold the island if at all possible. In looking over the options available to him, the President became aware that his "Tropic Lightning" 25th Division was already underway: headed to Australia and then to New Guinea. A diversion was promptly ordered, and the 25th Division rerouted and committed to the Battle of Guadalcanal. General Collins, commanding the Tropic Lightning Division, became known as "Lightning Joe" – a nickname which was to stick for the rest of his life.

# Marine Corps Mentors:
# Advice to the Fresh Troops

Our Marine Corps mentors met and stayed with us full time for the few days we had them. Casually, but firmly, they gave of their experiences, learned a hard way in fighting the Jap. They told us to be aware of their cleverness, such as placing explosive charges called "booby traps" inside enticing objects: things which a soldier might take a fancy to. These would explode when picked up, killing or maiming their enemy. They told of a Jap surrendering while concealing a grenade which he would use to kill an enemy (and himself). A Jap sniper would climb high into the crown of a coconut tree, tie himself in place, and proceed to kill by sniping the Marines. Tree-hidden snipers were hard to locate and were successful in taking a considerable toll. At night, a Jap might infiltrate a Marine position and start calling "Corporal of the Guard," in English. When receiving a reply, it helped the Jap to locate and eliminate another Marine. Accordingly, we were told to never reply to such calls. Instead, we were to seek out the caller and, making use of the rifle-mounted bayonet, silence the enemy. "Never," said our Marine, "never be taken prisoner. You will be awful sorry and, eventually, awfully dead if you permit yourself to be taken prisoner. Much better to fight it out to the death, and much less painful. And always remember that the only good Jap is a dead Jap."

We were advised further. "Always try to carry two canteens of drinking water, and never take a drink from any stream – or otherwise, well…you will find out why soon enough; and," our mentor added: "always carry as many hand grenades as you are comfortable with. Now, we all know that the hand grenade has a short, three-second fuse before it explodes, but you will be surprised at how many times one can be thrown back-and-forth in three seconds. I always pull the pin, let the handle fly off to start the fuse burning, and hold it, ready to throw, for a long second before throwing it at the enemy. This is a more certain way to get him. But remember: don't hold it too long, and always be sure to throw it!"

We learned that aviation gas was in such short supply that we could not put up fighter planes at night. Vehicles were in such short supply that artillery pieces were being moved by manpower. Rations were short. All this, because our supply ships had been halted midway during the offloading, and ordered out of the area to prevent them being sunk or destroyed by the enemy.

We learned that, back on New Caledonia, U.S. troops were acutely aware of the shortages on Guadalcanal. They were taking it upon themselves to steal jeeps and prime-mover trucks, food, and barrels of aviation gas; these they took to the waterfront, and loaded aboard any naval vessel heading north whose commanding officer would agree to accept the cargo. No one had ever heard of offered stolen-goods or equipment being refused. Thus, a black-market supply effort came into being, much to the fervent appreciation of the beleaguered American troops on the awaiting end.

The Marine sergeant who was with our group broke out a map which he had made, and proceeded to brief us with the following information:

"The island of Guadalcanal was a British protectorate, and was important for its coconut products used by Lever Brothers in their manufacture of soaps and related products.

"It is about five degrees south of the equator, with the long-axis roughly parallel to the equator. This long-side measures about 100 miles and the north-south distance measures about 30 miles. Henderson Field is midway on the north side of the island.

"Along the coast are mile after mile of coconut groves, which extend inland as much as a mile. Also along the coast are mangrove swamps, which are extremely difficult to penetrate. A mountain range runs parallel to the long-axis of the island and reaches a height of 7,600 feet. Perpendicular to the central range are many volcanic ridges extending toward the ocean. The valleys between the ridges are almost solid jungle with a stream running full at the bottom of each. Foot paths largely follow these streams, but some are in the jungle and require much cutting away of vegetation to permit movement. The jungle is full of birds of all kinds, monkeys, and other jungle creatures. Treeless areas are covered by coarse grass about six feet high.

"There had been Catholic and Protestant missions on the island, and mission sailing-vessels for transportation. The missionaries left, taking women and children with them. Those who failed to leave were mostly killed by the Jap, but a few came over to the Marines and received safe keeping. The remaining men are more or less under the control of the British colonial officer who also serves as a "coast watcher," observing enemy movements and reporting them to Australia by radio.

"When the Marines landed, the objective was to seize control of the airfield being constructed by the enemy and complete the construction for use by Marine and Navy air forces. This they did – taking and securing a perimeter from the northern beach, back and around the airfield, and back to the beach again. This area is about six miles long and three miles deep. It is strongly secured, but enemy patrols do succeed in filtering through. Large enemy units have been attacking in strength – attempting to break through and retake the American-held zone. There have been many and continuing battles all around this perimeter.

"Several miles to the west, along the north shore also, Japanese regularly land fresh troops and supplies – even in broad daylight. All the rest of the island is a "no man's land" with strong patrol-activity: from both sides, all over the place. In this no man's land, there are apparently no fixed bases or camps."

We listened, asked questions, and soaked up the knowledge like sponges. Our sergeant was great!

Figure 26. Map of Guadalcanal Island (US Army)
reprinted from *The 25th Division and World War 2* (p 22),
Cpt. Robert F. Karolevitz, ed., 1946, Army and Navy Publishing Co.

# Uniforms: A Dilemma

Interestingly, we had no battle uniforms. We each had blue "fatigue" work clothes (which would show like a flag against the green jungle); "suntans;" and a pair of green, gas-impregnated coveralls, treated to protect against gas attack. These were the right color, but were so heavy, hot, and smelly that it was not possible to use them. We each tried washing our coveralls in soap and water many, many times – attempting to make them usable, but to no avail. Thus, we adopted the use of suntans for our daily clothing. By now, from wearing the least clothing possible when on board ship, we were brown as could be – and whenever possible, we went with the least clothing acceptable.

# Atabrine

While still aboard ship, we each began taking daily Atabrine tablets, designed to protect against malaria during the period taken. They gave protection, but not immunity. Also, they gave a yellow cast to one's skin. Sergeant McKee stood at the head of the battery chow line, personally issued a tablet to each man every day, and saw to it that it was taken. A few men cleverly tried to avoid taking and swallowing their tablet for personal reasons of rebelliousness. In time, they could be identified by their non-yellow skin.

# The Night before Embarking on Guadalcanal

I don't recall how much I slept the night before we went ashore. My gear was packed and ready to go long ahead of time, as was that of all the others. The mess was open all night. We were advised to eat well, because it would be a long time before another meal…and that would be of a much different quality. Thus, breakfast in the middle of the night was not eggs and pancakes: it was steak and all that went with it. Although ever so good, I didn't feel all that hungry.

From the deck in the early-morning darkness, I could see the island mountain range as our ship moved along parallel to it. Yet still dark, "general quarters" was sounded, telling each of us to return to our assigned sleeping quarters below deck. There, I tried my pack on and made adjustments so that it carried as well and securely as possible; adjusted the sling of my rifle so it fit diagonally across my shoulder: butt down and muzzle up – giving it the least opportunity to hang up during the climb down the cargo net. I noticed that the other men had arrived at the same solution also. Backpack and rifle were then stowed again on my bunk, and I engaged in monotone conversation with those who were just around me. The conversation, I do not recall. Our new first sergeant, Sergeant Bowman, and the brass noncoms walked casually up one aisle of bunks and down the next, engaging each man in quiet and reassuring conversation as they went. I remember that it gave me a good feeling: encouraged that all would be going well for us. Neither Bowman, nor any of the others, had done anything like this before either, but they showed cool and thoughtful heads.

# Boarding the Higgins Boat:
# Ashore on Guadalcanal

I believe that we did not drop anchor when the ship's propulsion system stopped. This was either because the water was too deep, or possibly to allow for hasty departure if needed. In the stillness, we waited below for our turn on deck. I don't recall how long we waited, but believe that we were among the early units to depart. A Navy bosun and our first sergeant took charge and quietly passed word that we were moving up to our position on deck. From there, we would go over the side and down the cargo nets into the Higgins boats waiting below. We were cautioned to keep our footing, to hold fast with our hands while descending, and in no case to fall from the net, since we were most likely in deep water.

Slowly we moved out, aisle after aisle, found our ladder and moved upward – coming out at last onto the main deck. Here, the air was fresh and welcome. There was no time to look around, just move across in line to our position at the railing. I had a moment to look down at those already in the process of descending. The small boats below rose and fell in the water, but the ocean was smooth. "OK, DREW, your turn." Sergeant Bowman touched me on the shoulder. "Hold tight and be careful; you'll have no trouble." With that, I gripped the ship's railing, swung a leg over, and felt about with my foot for the waiting horizontal line of the cargo-net mesh. Finding it, I brought my other leg over the railing and, continuing to hold fast to the bar, began my descent: step after step, hand grip after hand grip. The waiting Higgins boat grew larger, and then a helping hand reached me from below. I stepped onto the Higgins railing and lowered myself down to the bottom, which was some five feet below. No problem at all, just…"Do it as we practiced back on Hawaii!"

The Higgins boats were plywood landing craft with a pointed bow. There was no ramp to let down, and each man had to mount up to the railing again to go over the side. The boat's bow was run up to the beach as much as possible, and kept there by the continuing forward thrust of the boat's propellers. Whatever load each man was responsible for was carried in the backpack; and this – plus rifle, ammunition, steel helmet, and sheathed bayonet – went up and over the side, then down into whatever depth of water remained below the boat's bottom. It was perhaps waist deep. I don't recall.

As soon as I was in the water, I filed off to the shore – and on into the coconut grove beyond. Each unit had been assigned an area for assembly, and there we headed. As I walked, I recall seeing a lone soldier with rifle over his shoulder walking ever so slowly along the beach toward us. His face was blank of expression, his eyes were dull; he gave the impression of looking for a familiar face among the new arrivals. The thought crossed my mind that here was a man who had experienced too much, and who now needed help.

# Chapter 6.
# Guadalcanal – December 1942

## Setting Up

Perhaps a half mile inland from the beach, we arrived at the area temporarily staked out for our battery, and assembled by section. Each sharing our shelter-half with the half of another, we began pitching tents and cutting drainage trenches around them. No sound of battle whatever up to now! Work parties were quickly assembled for digging slit trenches wide enough and deep enough for body protection. Straddle trench latrines were dug and made ready for use.

Gordon and I put our two shelter-halves together, doubled our blankets into half-width, and placed them side by side. We then placed the rest of each backpack at the closed-end of the tent. The tent halves were fastened together by matching the buttons on one half with the buttonholes on the other. When set up, the tent was about four feet high at the ridge; it sloped to the ground on each side, where it was fastened by short, wooden pegs. The closed-end sloped from the ridge to the ground also, and it was this sloping, extra space which provided for our packs. The tent was about five feet wide from the stakes on one side to the stakes on the other side. We slept on the ground, with two thicknesses of blanket under us and one blanket each left for covering us for warmth should we need it.

Sergeant McKee had already raised a kitchen overhead-shelter, and had his field-ranges set up and working. He had several Lister bags set up, hanging from tripods, and was even now looking for a water point for drinking water. He passed the word for each man to drop his first day's ration off at the kitchen: One stack was for hash-brown potatoes and corned beef, another for beans and bacon, another for spam with eggs. We each kept our own candy and cigarettes – McKee cared not about that. Babcock had already raised the officers' mess tent by himself, and was now ready to look after the nourishment needs of his officer charges.

I felt glad that Sergeant McKee had made the effort to provide the men of the battery with a hot meal on our very first day ashore on Guadalcanal. There was plenty of coffee and even canned fruit for dessert. I marveled at his presence of mind and excellent organization, but should never have been surprised. Feeding the men of the battery, making sure each took his Atabrine, and making certain that each man kept his mess-gear sparkling clean was exactly what he was supposed to do. McKee had even encouraged his two lead-cooks to take up barbering – and that is what they did in their off-duty time. Ever in demand, they provided short haircuts to each man of the battery.

It was a long and busy day. Each section had found its particular equipment and brought it to their encampment area. The equipment for our group was small in quantity: two surveying transit instruments, two stadia rods, and two sets of surveying chains. This – along with rifles, ammunition, mess gear, water canteens, and notebooks – was all that we needed.

# First Night's Guard Duty

A Battery Headquarters tent was set up, complete with a bulletin board in front. Guard-duty rosters had already been made up, and were posted on the bulletin board. Guards would pull a two-hour shift before being relieved by the next guard-shift. Sentry posts were stationary, and were manned with loaded rifle and fixed bayonet. We were instructed in no case to fire a shot, nor make a vocal challenge. If someone was in our area who did not belong: "Use the fixed bayonet and do it silently." After guards were posted for the night, anyone other than the sentry and sergeant of the guard did not belong in the area.

It was dark when I accompanied Sergeant Barnes to my assigned post. There, he relieved the guard on duty who departed with him. "Don't move about," Barnes told me. "Remain quiet. Just watch and listen. I'll be back when your shift is half over to check up on you. And," he added, "don't worry: you'll not hear me, so don't worry about using your bayonet on the wrong person."

The night was dark, no moon at all – but my eyes did become used to the darkness, and I could see moderately well. Funny how the stumps assumed shapes and seemed to move in the darkness. High above in the coconut treetops, large-winged bats could occasionally be seen flying about. Now and then, a large coconut would break free and crash to earth with a heavy thud. The weight of the coconut and the height of fall seemed enough to kill a horse should it hit one. Time passed very slowly, but not monotonously. Suddenly, I became aware that Sergeant Barnes had returned, unseen and unheard, as he had said. He addressed me so quietly that I scarcely heard him. He told me that everything was going well, and that he would return next time with my relief. I began to really appreciate how very capable the senior section-chiefs were, and how unassuming they were in their conduct of duty.

I strained my eyes, watching the tricky coconut stumps as they seemed to move and shift shapes. Listen as I might, I could not locate a sentry to my right nor to my left – nor could I detect Sergeant Barnes as he made his rounds. Suddenly, a memory came flashing back to me: how I had observed the section chiefs at night in Hawaii as they went out beyond the battery area and walked about. They had been practicing! "Hell, Drew," I realized, "they were practicing and learning how to move about noiselessly. Well now, that was clever. I'm going to take time to practice how to move silently and unobserved too. And what better time to learn!"

When next he returned to my guard post, Sergeant Barnes brought my replacement, and I departed my post together with Sergeant Barnes. En route to our encampment, we were stopped by a wavering, but loud call: "Corporal of the Guard!" It went again, over and over: "Corporal of the Guard!" Then there was a thud like a coconut hitting the ground, followed by silence. Barnes and I moved on, making our way back to our bivouac. I was dismissed and found my way to the pup tent which I shared with Gordon. Gordon was sound asleep, and I doubt he even knew that I had returned. Crawling into my side of the tiny tent, I removed my steel helmet; lay my rifle in the space between us; and went to sleep. We were sleeping fully-clothed and ready for whatever might happen. Next morning at breakfast, Sergeant Barnes told us that the "Corporal of the Guard" incident in the night was by one of the officers who had come ashore with us. He had been taken unharmed, and was under care of the division medics for the moment.

# Settling In: Day Two

The second day on the island was spent moving from the beach to a more permanent, assigned area much further inland – near the inland-end of coconut groves. Jungle was just beyond. A dirt trail separated our Division Artillery Headquarters from Division Headquarters. We were the width of a city street between General Reinhart on our side, and General Collins on the other. In the past, we had never seen our general officers, now we saw them every day, and even many times each day.

In our new location, Sergeant Riley was probably the busiest. He began establishing a "motor pool" for the few trucks and jeeps we were receiving, and arranging a safe maintenance area separate from a safe fueling area. Corporal Shumway, head mechanic of the motor pool, was busy making sure that each of his vehicles was operational, fueled, and ready. Each vehicle also had an assigned driver – except for mess, survey, wire, and weather. For these, the section chief was personally responsible.

The second night ashore, I could see how the men were beginning to "sort themselves out." This, to me, meant that some were making the extra effort to improve, while others used any free time for simply relaxing and taking it easy. That second evening, I saw perhaps a dozen men off in the jungle edges practicing and learning "silent movement," as had been observed being done by Sergeant Barnes just the night before. These men were making an extra effort towards success in their war against the Jap. Needless to say, I was among those practicing.

# Third Day Ashore:
# Survey Work Begins In Earnest

Our third day ashore saw the survey section beginning work in earnest. It was our job to establish base lines, orienting lines, and exact points of known locations. We carried this data down to the headquarters of each of the four artillery battalions of the division. Each battalion had as their survey chief a captain or major who also served as the battalion operations officer. Although a sergeant, and younger in years than the battalion officers, Gordon was Chief of Survey for Division Artillery, and thus, technically senior to the others. It was interesting to me, in seeing them together with no one wearing insignia of rank, that Gordon was obviously the one in charge!

We broke into two survey parties: Gordon, Russell and I in one, and Corporal Ready, Walsh, and Wells in the other. We had already recognized that, being south of the equator, magnetic compasses manufactured for the Northern Hemisphere were useless. Because of this, all of our survey effort would have to be done by means of "triangulation." This involved shooting angles, measuring distances, and calculating the data using trigonometry and logarithmic tables. The results produced very accurate map data and allowed our artillery pieces to "fire for effect" with the first round fired! A remarkable achievement!

Gordon had already collected several expended, brass shell casings from a 105 mm battery. These empty shell casings were about four inches in diameter and eighteen inches long. They would be driven into the ground at primary survey-stations which we would occupy from time to time. We then could place a transit directly over the casing's center point when using the station. Gordon had a kit of steel punches, each with a letter or number. With these and a hammer, he would punch in a serialized number, letter, station, and elevation (above mean sea level).

104

We placed our first marker in the soil just off the runway of Henderson Field and the second marker exactly 1,000 yards down the runway, near the end toward the jungle. We chained the distance several times to obtain the closest-possible, accurate length of this first leg. This operation established one quite-exact side of a triangle, and could be used for limitless sizes and shapes for other triangles. With trigonometry – if you have two "known sides" and one angle of any triangle; or two angles and one side of any triangle – you can determine, with total accuracy, all other sides in length and all other angles in degree.

As a third point, Gordon selected a prominent, open hilltop. It was some distance away, yet still on the American-side of the perimeter. A shell casing was planted there and a transit set up over its center point. From here, we measured the horizontal and vertical angles to the other points at each end of Henderson Field and calculated the results. Now we had our first triangle. We knew exactly the length of each of the three sides; the exact degree in minutes and seconds of the three included angles; and the exact vertical distance of each point above sea level. From this hilltop vantage point, it was easy to read angles to other positions: All we needed was one new "direction reading" and a new "measured distance;" or, if possible, we could read angles from two known positions. That was enough to establish exact data on the new location.

With our transit, stadia rod, and chain, each party went everywhere, "surveying-in" enemy positions and carrying location data down to each of our artillery battalions. We could almost always depend on enemy snipers taking interest in our activities, and we did provide a good target as well! We also noticed that our infantry units disliked our presence in their areas, because it meant they would receive additional fire from the enemy.

Sergeant McKee had created a "blackout" tent which he kept in operation all the time. In front of the entry was a kind of closet with canvas curtains over two sides. Thus, you would walk into a black chamber, let the curtain fall behind you, and then enter into the tent by way of the second curtain. It worked well. Gordon set up shop there, and did all of his calculations at night. Sometimes the battalion survey officers were there with him; other times, he worked alone. As he grew in confidence that Russell and I could do satisfactory work, Gordon turned much of the calculating over to us. He then ran the check-up over our work. This gained him a little spare time to relax in the blackout poker-tent.

# Washing Machine Charlie

From the first night ashore, we had all become familiar with "Washing Machine Charlie" – a name given early on to a Jap Navy, flying-boat aircraft. It was so named because its twin engines seemed to be unsynchronized, with a resulting unharmonious sound: comparable to the sound of a washing machine in operation. Charlie came over almost every night. Our searchlights could reach up, capture Charlie, and follow him easily enough. Our anti-aircraft batteries did throw shells his way, but he was able to fly above the reach of our guns. Charlie would fly about, dropping bombs at his choosing. Then he would depart, only to revisit us the next night. His bombs did real damage. I have no idea how many American lives he claimed, but one grim night these bombs killed several of the men in my battery and sent many others to the hospital.

# Christmas Cheer

Remembering General Washington's famous "Christmas Attack" during the Revolutionary War, I fully expected all-out enemy assaults on our positions during the Christmas and New Year holiday season. General Collins was obviously of the same mind, and saw to it that all of our front-line infantry and all of our artillery were alert, reinforced, and ready for whatever the enemy might have planned for us. Also, General Collins intended that Christmas and New Year's be treated as special days for all the front-line troops. The order was given that all troops receive special holiday meals, and that all of them would be hot meals.

Thinking about it, I realized the magnitude of such an effort. I observed that Sergeant McKee's kitchen began preparing the special dishes for our company in the middle of the night. He had extra kitchen police and assistant cooks engaged in meal preparations, and served us "Chicken a la King" at the main meal. I had heard of such a dish, but never seen or eaten it before, and can tell you that it was a most savory dinner. I was awe-struck, thinking about how much work it must have been cooking this for over 200 lean and hungry men!

At the front-line positions all around the battle perimeter which I visited that day, I saw the same activities: field kitchens set up well forward of where they usually were, only a short walk from the very front line, and back below a protecting slope. Each unit obviously had a rotation-plan where one man would stay in position, while a partner was relieved to walk back to the field kitchen, and enjoy an excellent hot meal. The men I saw ate leisurely, and then returned to the front to relieve a partner who then came back for his hot meal. Believe me, hot meals were a rare experience for the men in the foxholes, mortar- and machine-gun emplacements. The General also had his regimental bands as close to the front perimeter as the field kitchens. There, they played music off and on, the whole-day long, for friend and enemy alike.

Action went on as usual Christmas Day with shooting and shelling from both sides, but no special all-out offensive as I had thought likely from the canny and treacherous Jap. Gordon, Russell, Walsh and I visited many of the forward infantry positions that day. Many of the infantrymen had come to know us and we were becoming friends with them. Gordon brought cigarettes along, which he passed out to anyone desiring an extra ration. I never knew how he had come by them, but in his position as Chief of Survey for the division, he had many high-level contacts – even with the Seabees – and was good at trading souvenirs for more desirable luxuries.

A one-page Christmas newsletter from General Collins was given to each of us. It told about how the war was going all over the globe, wished each of us a very happy holiday, and gave permission for each man in writing home to tell the folks where we were: "Lucky to be alive, and lucky to be on Guadalcanal!"

# Salting the Creek: Fool's Gold

A few weeks after we came ashore, our survey teams started going through our forward infantry lines and beyond into no man's land to locate and survey-in "targets of opportunity." In no man's land, Gordon would set his transit up on an open hilltop from which he could sight rearward onto one of our targets of known location. I always got the job of taking the eight-foot-tall stadia rod – with its red and white bull's-eye atop – down into some jungle-pocket of interest. Then Gordon would have to move his transit to another known location, and swing a second angle to my stadia rod. This accomplished, we had the new location recorded, and could take our business elsewhere.

Some nights, Gordon and I sat in our tent, each with a steel file from the motor pool, and made small, sparkling, gold-colored filings from expended rifle cartridges. When we had a cup full of filings, we selected a sandbank in the shallow water of the Tenaru River where we proceeded to "salt" the wet sand with our filings. A day or so later, Gordon showed a handful of the wet sand to Walsh. John Joseph Pershing Walsh could hardly contain himself in his excitement, and grilled Gordon at length until he had obtained the location of our finding. Thereafter, Walsh happily worked his "claim" with the aid of a shallow pan "borrowed" from the kitchen. His gleanings were impressive. He accepted our disinterest in panning for gold when Gordon told him, "Hell, Walsh...none of the survey crew are gonna survive the war. We'll most likely get killed right here on Guadalcanal. I ain't gonna spend a lot of time panning for gold under these circumstances, when I can have ever-so-much-more fun playing poker in my spare time." As I recall, no one ever told Walsh that he had been panning "fool's gold" instead of the real stuff.

Figure 27. "Wright Road looking north on Guadalcanal. This road was the chief supply thoroughfare during the campaign on that island." US Army photo reprinted from *The 25th Division and World War 2* (p 27), Cpt. Robert F. Karolevitz, ed., 1946, Army and Navy Publishing Co.

# The Jeep with a Mind of Its Own

On one particular day, four of us from survey section were in our jeep: Gordon at the wheel as usual. We were driving up the "safe side" of a considerable incline through the jungle, when an artillery-shell burst right in front of us. The jungle took the hit, but the jeep died right on the spot. Nothing Gordon could do would get the engine going again. We all got off and pushed and shoved. Finally getting the jeep turned around, we coasted back downhill for quite a distance. Arriving at the bottom of the ridge, Gordon tried the engine again and it took off perfectly.

Turning around again, Gordon made a second run at the slope and – no sooner did we reach the spot where the artillery shell had nearly reached us – the jeep died again. We repeated the process of turning around and going back downhill. At the bottom of the hill, the jeep cranked up just fine. A third run was made at the slope, but the jeep had a good memory. A fourth run was tried: same result. We gave up, pulled off the trail, took the distributor cap (which for a jeep is the same as the ignition key), and finished the hill on foot.

At the top of the ridge, we set up our survey gear, and proceeded to locate the targets which we had come for. While we were there, a sniper found us and proceeded to make life miserable for us. We also came under close mortar and artillery fire, and – equally bad: flying fragments of rocks from the shell explosions. All four of us were dinged up that day; most of mine, as I recall, was below the knees. We finished the survey and, with rock-torn slacks, made the hike back to the foot of the ridge and our waiting jeep. It cranked up just as it should, and we were soon back at the battery. We each reported in at the battery aid station where the medical officer and his assistants picked the imbedded debris out, swabbed the scrapes with Merthiolate, and sent us back to duty.

Our young medical officer had a Greek name: Stanipoulis – Captain George Stanipoulis. On another occasion, I was having trouble hearing; he spent quite a bit of time with me, and greatly helped in clearing up the problem. Here, we didn't have a "roll call" or a "sick call." If you needed something, you just went over to the aid station, told the corporal what it was, and you were taken care of – just like that. No waiting, no report, nothing.

There were times later on, when we took the jeep back to the hill it had refused to climb, and interestingly, it had a good memory. It never did go all the way to the top of the ridge. When it reached the place where it had received that near-miss from an artillery shell, it would always stop. Every time, we had to jigger it around and coast back to the bottom of the hill – and there, it would start up again just like it should. Finally, we simply gave up and stopped trying to get Gordon's jeep to go all the way to the top of that particular ridge. The work required to turn it around manually on a one-lane trail in the middle of the jungle was too much.

# Rank, Protocol, and Perks

Division Headquarters and Division Artillery Headquarters were right across a dirt vehicle-trail from each other. General Collins was at the former, and General Reinhart at the latter. Headquarters Company, consisting of some 200 enlisted men, supported General Collins. Headquarters Battery, with an equal number of enlisted men, supported General Reinhart. Each command had several staff officers as well. The enlisted men were under the control and supervision of the first sergeants and section chiefs. They had truly minimal contact with the officer personnel. Our battery had three officers who could be seen in their mess tent, but I don't recall a word ever passing between any of them and ourselves. Officer contact seemed limited to first sergeants, section chiefs, and no one else. I liked it that way.

In time, I became aware that both camps of officers had a "non-government issue" always available in the seclusion of their portion of camp: liquor. Somehow too, I learned that they had one officer who made regular flights to New Caledonia and New Zealand, where he procured the varieties and quantities of liquor desired by those involved. The Seabees (U.S. Navy Construction Battalion) had beer – **cold** beer – cold soda pop, and even ice cream. But the "GIs" – the enlisted men of the U.S. Army on the island – wouldn't have recognized beer or pop had we seen it. It just wasn't available to us, and we never even talked about it.

# A Feast to Remember

The Quartermaster Company had the job of maintaining adequate "dumps" of all supplies needed by all the units of the division. A "dump" was an outdoors compound surrounded by high, barbed-wire fences with a guarded gate for entry, and another guarded gate to exit. The ration truck would enter, make one circular pass through the compound while loading provisions, and then go on to the exit. There was no "shopping-around," and no second-pass through. Each mess sergeant would have in hand his copy of a printed list of what he could draw that day, and what quantities he could draw. The list was checked by the guard on the exit gate before the driver was allowed to proceed. The supply truck was the kind used for towing artillery pieces: it was big and had a six-wheel drivetrain. When he was ready for a "supply run," Sergeant McKee would "volunteer" whomever seemed available at the moment as labor to load the provisions. McKee was never short of volunteers, because the trip always included a treat of some kind, not otherwise available.

I don't recall how it was that I was available, but was part of the ration detail on one occasion. McKee drove to the food-ration dump, gained entrance, dropped off one of the cooks, and began his circuitous route. Food was in stacks twice as high as our truck, each stack a separate item. On this trip, he was mostly interested in canned fruit and dried fruit of any kind, and sugar - lots of sugar. On top of these items, he had us carefully arrange cases of spam, cases of peas in gallon cans, cases of dehydrated cabbage, butter, and fifty-pound bags of flour. Reaching the exit gate, McKee waited for the cook, who was busy telling GI stories with the guard and trading enemy souvenirs. The guard casually looked our load over and waved us through the gate.

Arriving back at the battery position, McKee had us offload the truck. The more valuable items were carefully arranged and stored to prevent pilfering. That same day, we made another run to a different supply-compound, and all we obtained were a lot of five-gallon water cans. That evening, McKee had a meeting with the section chiefs.

Before the Jap came and took over the island, the copra plantations were well-organized and efficiently managed. Each plantation had a stable of riding horses and pastures of cattle. With the arrival of the Jap, the plantations stopped working and became deserted. The native men left for the hills. The women and children left the island on board missionary sailing vessels, which dropped them off at other islands left unoccupied by the Japs. I never saw any horses; perhaps they were valuable enough to have been removed to safety. The cattle simply wandered off from the pasture areas and, thereafter, were only seen occasionally. They would do their grazing early in the morning or late in the evening, and spend the rest of the day lying down in concealing shade, munching their cud.

Early one morning, I saw Sergeant McKee and Corporal Ratliff, one of the cooks, as they were driving away from the motor pool in a weapons carrier. "Strange," I thought. "Why are they driving-off towing an engine hoist? What in the world would the mess sergeant be doing with an engine hoist? Also, why the weapons carrier instead of the six-wheel drive truck?"

While they were gone, the other cook, Corporal Webster, had some of the men gather a stack of coconut logs and dig a pit about two feet wide, six or eight feet long, and three feet deep. In this, he began a roaring fire which slowly reduced to the hottest bed of coals I had ever seen. As I watched in curiosity, I saw Motor Sergeant Riley and Chief Mechanic Sergeant Shumway drive up and offload a windlass, which they had manufactured from truck axles and other parts. This, under Corporal Webster's direction, was placed lengthwise over the pit.

114

About this time, I saw Sergeant McKee and Corporal Ratliff driving up to the first aid station, where they found the medical officer. After a short conversation, the medical officer followed them to the weapons carrier and began checking a skinned and gutted beef-cow, obviously checking if it was fit for dinner; and apparently, the beef passed. A few eager hands were enlisted to offload the animal, place it on the windlass, and secure it there with tire chains to prevent it from falling off.

By now, everyone around had figured it out. McKee and Ratliff had been away hunting dinner for us. Willing hands were available to slowly turn the spitted beef, while Webster and Ratliff, using new cotton mops, swabbed the roasting carcass from buckets filled with McKee's very own homemade barbecue sauce. I learned from all this that it takes a long time to barbecue a beef over a pit of red-hot coals. I also learned that the end result is truly worth every bit of effort!

For dinner that night, the battery had guests: General Collins and ten or twelve officers from his headquarters, and General Reinhart and ten or twelve officers from his headquarters. Since it was his battery hosting the event, Captain Kadick led the chow line. Next came our two generals, followed by the staff officers. Each officer had his field mess gear, and I noticed that each knew how to properly hold the skillet and lid, and the canteen cup. Each gave his preference of cut to a smiling Sergeant McKee, who personally served them. Having been well-served, they departed to their area to eat. Our First Sergeant Bowman was next in line, leading the enlisted men of the battery in no particular order. It was a feast I would never have dreamed of, carried out during the ongoing battle for Guadalcanal.

# Chaplain Mosley Joins Our Crew

I have no idea how many chaplains were attached to us. I only knew of one: Chaplain Mosley, a Protestant minister who came from the hill country of Tennessee. Now a captain in the Chaplain Corps, he worked out of our headquarters and had come to know of the survey crews. He was aware that our work too often took us into enemy territory, and involved more than a considerable risk to ourselves. General Collins also knew of our work, the great value of our maps for use in directing artillery concentrations, and the hazards which our surveying presented to each of us. General Collins always knew when we were out, and would personally check to learn that we had again returned. Chaplain Mosley decided that he would like to accompany us when we would be "out" in enemy territory for several days. He asked, and gained, permission from Gordon and from General Collins. Mosley turned his chaplain's steel helmet in for a regular one having no identifying markings on it. He already had a rifle of his own, and was known to be a crack shot. Mosley would be a welcome reinforcement should we get involved in a firefight.

Our job was to locate enemy positions and obtain information on their locations. We were to steer clear of any actual contact with the enemy if at all possible. At times, we went right up to the edge of a camp or installation, but we had been lucky to come and go unobserved. On the trip with Mosley along, we went a considerable distance into the Jap "Rear Area," far enough that we could identify the location of their long-range artillery. We knew that we were visible to anyone who looked our way. To appear innocent, we even made a fire at night, hoping to give the impression that we were a Jap unit out on patrol. After dark, we could see and hear their long-range artillery as it attacked our perimeter. The shells would whistle and swish while approaching and passing overhead. We would count the time between seeing the flash of the explosion at the target and hearing the explosion from the burst. This was an easy way to judge the distance between ourselves and our friendly lines. We had no other enemy contact.

Figure 28.  An example of the jungle's dense foliage.
US Army photo reprinted from *The 25ᵗʰ Division and World War 2*
(p 20), Cpt. Robert F. Karolevitz, ed., 1946, Army and Navy Publishing Co.

On the return trip, we had to penetrate and cross through the dense jungle valleys and the inevitable, fresh stream flowing at the bottom of each. It was in these areas that the unavoidable patrol-clashes would occur. The lucky patrol would be the one that spotted the other first. They would have the chance to prepare and ambush the other. These clashes were sudden, short, and violent. Passing through one jungle pocket, we came upon a full stream of running, fresh water – so inviting and tempting. Nevertheless, we elected to avoid splashing ourselves or sipping the fresh water. A few minutes later, we could hear the activity of the tens of millions of maggots. First you could always hear, then smell, and lastly see what lay before you: the violent firefight of a couple of hours earlier. An American patrol got the drop on a Jap patrol. Bodies lay in, or partially out of, the water – already green and badly bloated. They would soon be reduced to clothing-clad skeletons. We found no American dead, and hurriedly passed through and beyond.

While still in no man's land, we were welcomed by two enterprising Marine cooks. They had set up a field range under the shade of a shelter-half suspended on four stakes. They were providing hot coffee and fresh donuts to any and all returning patrols!

# Casualties and War Weary

Every day would see large numbers of our infantry going by on the way to the front perimeter, where they would dig in as reinforcement to the perimeter. As they passed our area, they were still fresh, well-fed, and carrying a full pack each. As the day wore on and grew hotter and more humid, they would begin to tire. Many would begin discarding things from their pack to lighten their load. It was more than sad to see the discarded litter and the wide range of items involved. It led me to consider that, among those going to the front, many were sorting themselves out to fail in their inevitable first-encounter with the enemy. This feeling was confirmed to me each evening before sunset, when trucks would be returning from the front, laden with the bodies of many men who had gone out that same morning, or perhaps the morning before. The trucks would go past our area and down to the island cemetery, where the flag never set. There, each man was given a clean, cotton mattress-cover as a last item of issue before being placed in his grave. How my heart went out to the men of the graves-registration detail, and their never-ending job of identifying, recording, and burying each man.

The only thing harder for me to witness was the lonely, solitary grave of one of our men, killed in the jungle off in no man's land. Since there was no way to return his body to the island cemetery, he was buried where he fell. Two broken sticks were placed on the grave in the form of a cross, one dog tag was hung from the cross, and his steel helmet placed on top of the cross. In a day or so, we knew the jungle would close over the spot, leaving no trace. The other dog tag would be turned in at company headquarters by the returning patrol, from whence would begin the long, slow process of notifying the next of kin. In time, bodies from the island cemetery would be removed from the island and re-interred at a cemetery location known to be permanently under the control of the United States government.

I don't recall the frequency, but it rained an awful lot: cats, dogs, and coconuts. It never stopped or slowed the war, and never caused an alternate plan to be put in operation. When it rained, you made an effort to keep your clothing dry, to be used and appreciated when the rain stopped. On the front perimeter, you would find infantrymen in foxholes or in mortar and machine-gun entrenchments, with a shelter-half stretched flat overhead. These men would be dressed in boots and undershorts only. All the rest of their clothing would be bundled up and stashed in the driest place possible – maybe a shell casing for example. Open fires were made with cardboard shell casings and the unused portion of propulsion packages. These might be gunpowder bags for example, or the sheet-like layers from mortar shells. Both made the quickest and hottest fire imaginable. Our men became expert in short order on how much gunpowder it took to heat a canteen-cup of water. They were also well-schooled in the drastic safety-practices needed to avoid the singed fingers, missing eyebrows, and other really nasty burns which could result from misuse of the procedure.

The closer to the front you went, the more miserable the condition of our infantrymen. Amazingly, the more miserable the condition of the American GI, the more cheerful the attitude seen among them! I was always so very proud of our American fighting men, their cheerfulness and good humor…the back-

and-forth banter. Unless you were a part of it, it would have been impossible to imagine.

Out in no man's land, battles would involve small units, squads of six or seven men on each side, or platoon-size units of thirty-five or so on each side. These shoot-outs would be of short duration, and furious – followed by silence. Battles for position might involve a thousand enemy of battalion-strength, or a regiment-strength of three thousand men. These battles might last half a day, or sometimes two or three days, with large numbers of killed and wounded.

Figure 29.  Bivouac of 25th Division Troops near the front lines on Guadalcanal.  US Army photo reprinted from *The 25th Division and World War 2* (p 43), Cpt. Robert F. Karolevitz, ed., 1946, Army and Navy Publishing Company.

# The Battle of Mount Austen

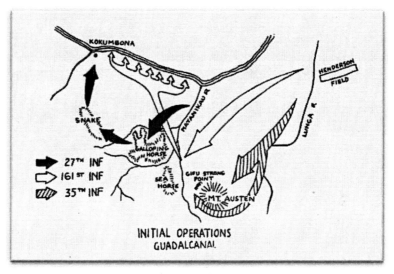

Figure 30. Initial Operations for the 27th, 35th, and 161st Infantry reprinted from *The 25th Division and World War 2* (p 26), Cpt. Robert F. Karolevitz, ed., 1946, Army and Navy Publishing Company. (US Army)

The Battle of Mount Austen lasted from 10 January until 23 January. Our Infantry ended up fighting on short rations and limited water supply. The native men, who served loyally in carrying supplies to the front, deserted entirely when the battle really heated up. This left the movement of supplies totally up to the infantry. Our dead and wounded could not be reached for some time, a situation of real concern to everyone.

In preparation for the Battle of Mount Austen, our little survey crew had the advance assignment. The four of us – Gordon, Russell, Walsh, and I – were not only loaded with our usual survey gear, but also, this time, with a backpack each of rations, extra water, extra ammunition, and hand grenades. We made our way through the jungle and up the ridges leading to Mount Austen. Sometimes we were seen by enemy snipers, who fortunately managed to miss us. On two or three occasions, we had mortar fire dropped on us, and were somewhat protected by the jungle from the flying shrapnel. A mortar shell gives no warning of approach. In open country, I might see the shell just before it exploded. In the jungle, however, the first clue is the sound of the explosion, the whistling of shrapnel, and the slashing of jungle growth.

Whenever we reached a position affording both a transit reading to an enemy target and also a back reading to known positions, we hurriedly set up and took the readings. Once we set up, it would have taken a direct hit on us to stop the reading. Close hits didn't count.

Behind us came our infantry, cutting their way through the jungle and establishing a perimeter line as they came. This consisted of laying down telephone line and digging fox holes, mortar- and machine-gun pits. These were then permanently manned. Each position was in sight of those to the right and left of it – which in the jungle, is five or ten feet apart. A single infantryman occupied each foxhole, and two or three men were in each mortar or machine-gun emplacement. The slow, struggling process of "advance and dig in" took several days, but finally the huge, jungle valley was completely surrounded and cut off by our infantry.

During all this time, the survey crew kept advancing and taking readings, which were sent back to the battery by radio. There, they were calculated out and turned into a very accurate firing-map for our artillery. During the process of encirclement, the Jap kept hitting our dug-in perimeter, but were never successful in breaking through. The fighting was grim and intense. It rained off and on, with an intensity only seen in the tropics. Soaked clothing only made you more miserable, so our men adopted the routine of stripping down during the rain, and keeping their clothing dry. They were somewhat protected by tent shelter-halves stretched over their foxholes or emplacements, and warmed by quick fires made of cardboard shell-boxes or unused, small bags of gunpowder.

The battle lasted for thirteen days. The last evening, loudspeakers were set up at intervals around the surrounded enemy. On the last morning of the battle, the speakers were turned on and a message in Japanese given to the enemy. "You are completely surrounded and cut off," it went. "You have thirty minutes from the time of this announcement to give yourselves up and surrender. If you surrender, you will be given prisoner status and will be well treated. The choice is yours."

Figure 31. "On 16 January 1943, two attempts to induce trapped Japanese to surrender were made via front line loudspeaker. Announcements were made in both English and Japanese, but no immediate results were forthcoming." US Army photo reprinted from *The 25th Division and World War 2* (p 30), Cpt. Robert F. Karolevitz, ed., 1946, Army and Navy Publishing Company.

Down in the depths of the dense jungle, there was silence for the longest thirty minutes; and then from far below, came the sound of a Jap bugle call. It was followed instantly by a violent attack up the slopes against our entire perimeter. The American response was instant and violent. I could see the enemy being beaten back into the depths of the jungle. Then came the most violent artillery shelling I had ever seen from the American guns far below. The intense bombardment was unceasing for ten minutes. When the shells burst, huge trees would rise up, severed by the explosions and lifted by concussion, then come crashing down.

The jungle was full of birds who rose in swarms into the air and made observation more difficult. With the artillery shelling, the enemy again rushed from the valley and fought their way up the slopes, only to be hurled back into the pocket below by the intense infantry-fire from the perimeter. Then again, came the blasting and bursting of artillery fire, which nothing could withstand. The Jap was desperate and determined. The Americans were not desperate, but were – if anything – even more determined.

When the artillery fire was finally lifted, a jungle valley in which visibility had been no more than five feet in any direction, looked like an Iowa cornfield after the hogs have devastated it. I could see every nick and corner in the huge valley below, which was probably a mile across. Then, with fixed bayonets, our entire infantry perimeter rose and advanced downward, into and through all the blasted jungle. There were occasional shots heard, some machine-gun fire still, but the entire valley was physically cleared out of enemy.

Returning back down the ridge, I came upon an American machine-gun emplacement. A warm fire was going, and the three Americans had a Jap with them. He was miserable and skinny, and was being given a hot ration and cigarette by the same men who would have shot him dead only minutes before.

The entire Japanese Oka Regiment was nearly wiped out in this battle, which is said to have "broken the back of the enemy's will to fight." In another short, four weeks, the Battle of Guadalcanal would be over. The men of the 35th Infantry, and those supporting the battle, were given a Presidential Unit Citation in recognition of all that they had gone through. It was the equivalent of a Distinguished Service Cross for every man engaged in the battle.

As we retraced our way back down the open ridge toward the battery, I could hardly believe the experiences of the past several days: the explosive violence, the utter devastation, and the Japanese dead everywhere. Our crew had gone ahead of the infantry by several days and, all told, were out some three weeks. We had no soap or towel, no razor, no change of clothing, and our only baths the drenching of the intermittent, downpouring rain. Fortunately, our field rations included cigarettes and, more importantly, toilet paper – or that would have been an even rougher experience.

I didn't feel exhausted by the heavy activity of the past three weeks. In fact, I don't recall that I ever felt exhausted or completely worn out in all the time that I was on the island. I believe that at least part of the credit belonged to Sergeant McKee and the all-out effort that he made in giving us the very best of Army rations, well prepared and appealing...plenty of hot food each and every day.

**Figure 32.**
**Larry at Guadalcanal**
**(Personal Photo)**

## A Welcome Back after Three Weeks Behind the Front Lines

Upon arriving back at the battery, the first thing we each did was stow our packs and gear where we slept. Then we each got a steel helmet full of hot water from the mess tent, returned to our pup tents, and enjoyed an allover wash and shave. We certainly looked dirty and shaggy after our three weeks in and behind the front lines. Next was a change of clean and dry clothing beginning with socks and underwear, shirt and slacks. We also each had a second pair of clean, dry shoes. Clean and now comfortable, I made my way to Sergeant McKee's mess tent for a welcome and enjoyable hot meal: all I cared for, of course, and good, hot coffee.

As usual, Sergeant McKee welcomed us back and sat with the four of us, asking questions and bringing us up-to-date on all that had been going on at the battery area during our absence. There had been rumors that Gordon had been killed, that Walsh had been wounded, and that no one knew where Russell and I were. It wasn't much later that the four of us made our way back to our pup tents, where we were soon sound asleep.

# Recommendation to West Point

A few days after the battle for Mount Austen was over, I was sitting alone in the mess tent when Gordon came along and joined me. It was obvious that his arrival had purpose and was not accidental. "I have news for you," he began. "Sometime toward the end of February, you are scheduled to leave the battery. Let me explain: The division commanders have been told to select two men from their division for West Point. General Collins and the brass have decided that you will be one of the two men named. And," he added, "I agree with them. The feeling is that if anyone can make the grade there, you have the most promise. Congratulations!" Gordon extended his hand.

News such as this was certainly the furthest from my mind, and diverse thoughts flooded my thinking process. Only a short time earlier, I had received a letter from my mother reminding me that I had enlisted while underage. I had not received my parents' consent to enlist, and I had abandoned my defense job without a release. The Army was slow in catching the error, but they did, and now were asking my parents' consent for my being in service. This was being withheld until they checked with me. "...Are you sure that you want to be in the Army?" they wrote. No answer would be given from them until they heard from me. While my parents were offering to pull me out of the Army, I had been well-received by the men of my battery, and had only the best of thoughts and experience for my association with them. Even now, engaged in the first American counter-offensive of the war against the Japs, I wanted to stay with the men whom I was fighting with and for whom I held the highest regard. Yet now, a second avenue was opening to me – again, leading out of combat!

Gordon's news initiated much soul-searching on my part. Frankly, I told him that the possibility of an Army career had never, ever entered my mind, and perhaps I was not the best choice. Gordon reasoned that I was not supposed to make such

127

a commitment – that all I was supposed to do was matriculate and graduate. After being commissioned, I would have a period of obligation and then could do whatever I wished. He thought it a great opportunity, and advised that I take every advantage of it. He assured me that those who had selected me would feel the same as he.

What unbelievable turns the winds of fate choose. First I find myself at Pearl Harbor – even though I had never initiated any paperwork to get me there. Now from the Battle of Guadalcanal, I am to be lifted and returned to the U.S. – again with no initiating action from me! What else had fate in store for me? I wondered.

Had the choice been offered to Gordon, he would have thought he had "…died and gone to heaven," he assured me. He was "pleased as all get-out" that it was going to me. He left and took a favorable report back to the brass – none of whom had even seen me, let alone made mention of what they had been thinking.

## Encouragement from the Battery

News of my impending departure was already circulating throughout the battery. The men would come by on their own to express their feelings: "Glad you're getting a chance to get out of this hellhole," one said. "If I had to pick someone for this assignment, you're the one I'd pick. Do a good job for us!" said another. Some would bring a letter for me to mail home for them when I reached Stateside; others would tell me of a favorite bar or restaurant. No one begrudged the thought that I might one day be an officer among them. Rather, they regarded me as a friend and future friendly contact in the Officer Corps! I had been in the battery a little over six months, and was touched beyond words at the total welcome, acceptance, and goodwill of each man. Who was I, and what could I have possibly done to merit all this? The bond was unbelievable! One had to actually live the experience in order to understand that.


# The *USS DeHaven*

From now until sometime in February, it was business as usual – each day bringing a different survey need and experience. One day we were running a survey along the beach, across swollen and swift-moving rivers, through coconut plantations, across saltwater marshes, and thence into jungle pockets. The next day could take us up to the perimeter to look for the source of incoming mortar and artillery fire. Here we always found the inevitable, well-hidden sniper, and knew that he would be shooting at us. In combat, there is no such thing as a day off!

On February 1, 1943, Gordon, Russell and I had made our way deep into enemy territory looking for hostile artillery and infantry positions, as well as ammunition and supply dumps. We set up our transit atop a barren, volcanic, rocky ridge from which we could look into the jungle and all around for hostile activity. To the north was the ocean, some four or five miles away, and beyond was Tulagi Harbor on Florida Island. A droning sound made its way into our conscious minds, growing ever-louder in intensity. A flight of enemy bombers appeared, coming in low over the ocean. From our elevated position, we looked down at them.

Just beyond was an American destroyer, steaming on a glass-like ocean toward Tulagi. We followed the action through the transit. The bombers, as one, bent their path to include the destroyer. As the flight passed above it, one plane was seen to release bombs. We saw the destroyer disappear from our view as it became utterly enveloped within a mountain of grey smoke, fires raging from its center. The enemy flight continued on, passing over our perimeter, where they thoroughly plastered our infantry and artillery positions with bombs. Back at the destroyer's position, the smoke and flame began to clear and we saw absolutely nothing where the vessel had been! Not even a ripple on the ocean! It was as though it had never been there!

Having released their bombs, the enemy flight turned inland toward the mountains and then, circling, came back toward the ocean. Closer and ever-closer to our position they came – then, they saw us! As one, the flight moved closer and closer toward our ridge. We could see the pilots' faces and mustaches, their waving and pointing arms and hands! We could almost reach out and touch them. And then as they flew by, the sons of bitches each in turn released their machine guns on us! We had no holes to jump into, no rocks to dive behind. We were out in the open as our work demanded; but we sure made the lowest-possible, horizontal profiles we could!

Rocks and debris were flung all about us! They were flying full-speed, but it seemed to us that it took them all day to pass us by! And then they were gone – back to the north from whence they had flown: Bougainville, their air base was called. We each stood up and were surprised that, amid so much action, we were still unhurt other than cuts and bruises from flying rock.

"Man!" said Gordon. "Man, I've never gone to church in my life! I've never said a prayer! In fact...I don't know *how*! But, if I ever get out of this place, I'm sure going to start!"

In fact, he did make it out alive, but just barely! I met him in San Francisco the following August. He told me then about a night time bombing raid that had demolished his tent and killed several of our buddies. After that, he did learn how to pray and began going to church.

Fifty years later, I learned the identity of the destroyer sunk that day. It was the *USS DeHaven*, the last American ship sunk in the Battle of Guadalcanal, which lasted from August 1942 through February 1943. The *DeHaven* had only just been commissioned in September of 1942, and may have been one of the destroyers escorting our division to Guadalcanal that November. On the afternoon of February 1, 1943, only 133 days after being commissioned, the *USS DeHaven* was hit by four bombs and sank very quickly. One hundred sixty-eight of her officers and crew were killed, including her captain, Commander Charles E. Tolman.

Figure 33. *USS DeHaven* passing North of Savo Island off of Guadalcanal on 30 January 1943. US Navy Photo 80-G-284577

# Shumway's "Croc"

Corporal Walter Shumway was the head mechanic in the Motor Section. He was a big man in his very early twenties – tall and big. He was strong enough to be able to lift the front end of an Army vehicle off the ground by himself. Fortunately for the rest of us, Shumway was friendly and easygoing, always ready for a laugh, even if it was at his own expense. It was Shumway and, to a lesser extent, his boss, Sergeant Riley, who kept all of the equipment in the motor section in top-notch, ready-to-go condition. There were other mechanics in the section too, but they all took their instruction from Shumway.

In earlier times, those few persons like Shumway would be found at the nucleus of the small settlements which seemed to naturally grow up around the Shumways of the world. They were the men who could, and did, do everything. They were the village blacksmiths, making everything from plowshares and wagon-wheels to rifles and guns for the men of the frontier.

One late afternoon, while at dinner in the mess tent and during a lull in the conversation, Shumway caught the attention of everyone in the mess tent at the time. "You know," he said casually, "I've been spending a little time early in the morning over there at that saltwater marsh. There's lots of critters down there: little deer, some monkeys, and birds of course, birds of all kinds, all over the place. And," he added quietly, "if you watch real careful, you will see a big crocodile moving slowly about and then, in a flash, he will rush out and grab for breakfast some critter he has had his eye on…while not being watched himself. Yes sir, there's a lot of action going on all the time over there at that saltwater marsh."

The men sitting around Shumway, listening to him, reacted as one:

"Boy, Shumway, that's a good one."

"How long did it take you to dream up that story, Shumway?"

"You always were a good storyteller, Shumway, but do you really expect us to believe this one?"

"Hell, Shumway, there ain't no crocs around here. They are only in Georgia, Florida, and Mississippi; and they are called 'gators,' not 'crocs,' Shumway!"

Shumway heard the men out, then responded to the group: "I knew, before I started to tell you about that saltwater marsh, that none of you would believe me; that's why I thought so long before mentioning it. All the same, I've told you. And if I was you, I'd be careful around that saltwater marsh, or you just might find yourself being somebody's breakfast. There, I've told you – now you guys are on your own!" From then on, Shumway's story made the rounds of conversation among the men in the battery; and everyone, it seemed, was of the same mind: "Shumway and his tall story."

Not many mornings later, the battery awoke with a crash. There was a huge din: shouting, crashing, splashing – unrecognizable sounds, all coming from the direction of the saltwater marsh. I was a light sleeper so I was one of the first who made it to the marsh. And such a sight! Shumway was mud from head to foot. Seeing me, he gave a grin. "Man, I'm sure glad to see you, Kid. Here, give me a hand so I can straighten up." He was grunting, heaving, and being shaken about like he was standing right in the middle of a Guadalcanal earthquake. He had both hands on a towrope which he had secured around his middle. The other end was securely looped over the jaws of the biggest (and only) 'crocodile' I had ever seen. The croc was thrashing, lunging, sweeping his huge tail, and trying hard to make it back into the marsh.

Several of us got thoroughly mud-encrusted and dinged up a bit before we had that monster tied-up until he couldn't move at all. Only then could we begin to release Shumway from the rope which he had looped about himself. The rest of us drug Shumway's prize back to the battery to be put on display, while a near-exhausted Shumway made it back slowly under his own steam. It took a bit of washing in the ocean to get rid of the mud; our clothes were left underwater, held down by chunks of corral, to let the surf soak in and do as much cleaning as possible. Then we made it to the mess tent for all the breakfast we could eat, while Shumway, surrounded by a battery of listeners, told us once again of his adventure with the crocodile.

# American Spam

Back in the civilian world of the United States, food companies were busy designing and packaging rations for individual soldiers. Each man would be given one of these ration boxes every day. Inside he would find a breakfast meal, a noon meal, and an evening meal. Also included would be a tiny box of four cigarettes, a paper folder of matches, a small folder of about a dozen sheets of toilet paper, and a tiny bar of soap. All food could be eaten cold, of course, but some meals were much better if heated – and eaten hot. One of these in particular was a tinned product identified by the manufacturer as SPAM. I'm uncertain of just what the ingredients of SPAM were, but appeared to be primarily pulverized, cured ham mixed with lots of fat. Hot or cold, it tasted pretty good – pretty good, that is, until I had only SPAM to eat morning, noon, and night for so long that I can't remember. In time, I came to relish it less and less, and finally to hate it. I found in talking and listening to others, that they seemed to feel the same as I.

Sergeant McKee really struggled with turning spam into a more savory meal for us, and was really inventive about it. We would get "spam and eggs" which was spam mixed with dehydrated eggs, served looking like patters of sausage. McKee devised a meatloaf-looking dish containing spam, bread crumbs, dried eggs, and you-name-it. We were served spam and cheese: a slab of spam with a thick slice of cheese melted over the top. There was baked spam, broiled spam, stewed spam, creamed spam over toast, hot spam sandwiches, cold spam sandwiches, spam and bacon, spam with creamed vegetables, even spam hash – and one we called "camouflaged spam."

For unit messes, rations were packaged in much larger portions. Spam was thus also put up into large, five-pound tins. Fruit came in one-gallon cans, and I remember peaches, pears and cherries. Also, peas came in one-gallon cans. Dehydrated potatoes and cabbage came in five-gallon, square cans. Butter from Australian was in one-gallon cans, and was as thick and hard as axle grease. I don't think that even a blowtorch could have melted it. The Australian-sourced butter was, of course, "reverse lend-lease."

## "Uncle Sugar" and British "Pork"

I remember seeing the local British Colonial Office official – dressed in clean, white shirt, walking shorts, knee-length socks, and tropical helmet – strolling through the coconut groves. He was noticeably making a count of downed coconut trees. This thoroughly intrigued me, and I set out to learn what he was doing. Hard for me to believe, but the Brit was taking count of all missing trees in order to bill the United States Government for them. Didn't matter who knocked them down, whether Jap, American, or Australian gunships, the U.S. paid the bill. Incongruous as it may have been, the U.S. Government had no way to charge the British for taking their island back from the Japs for them. "Lend-lease," it seemed, was really a one-way street – with "Uncle Sugar" picking up the bill.

# Chapter 7.
# New Caledonia

## Leaving the Battery at Guadalcanal

Toward the latter part of February 1943, the day came when I was to leave the battery and Guadalcanal for New Caledonia. My orders stated that I was to report to the President of the West Point Examining Board where I would be testing. Taking only a change of clothing and my shaving kit, I turned all other equipment and gear in at the battery supply tent and departed with Sergeant Joe Clark's good wishes. I checked through the mess tent for a handshake and a good luck from Sergeant McKee, and then made my way to the battery headquarters tent and Sergeant Hayes, the battery clerk.

Sergeant Hayes had my orders already prepared, and also had an official-looking Army folder which he gave me. "These are all of your records," he told me. "Turn them in at your next duty station. However," he added, "should you be tired of Army life and find yourself in Australia or New Zealand, you could simply go civilian and no one would be the wiser. You have all the Army's records that exist on yourself right now." Sergeant Hayes shook my hand and wished me good luck. My other friends in the battery had already said their goodbyes and gone off on their duty assignments. Outside the battery headquarters tent, a jeep and driver waited to take me to Henderson Field and drop me off. My departure was as quiet and inconspicuous as had been my arrival into the battery.

# The Flight to New Caledonia

At Henderson, there was a DC-3, twin-engine transport, waiting on the runway for departure to New Caledonia. I presented myself to the crew chief, a Marine sergeant, at the loading ramp, his clipboard in hand. My name was on his list and he checked it off, waving me to board. "Find yourself a seat," he told me. "We are just about to leave."

This was a new experience for me. I had never been inside an airplane before. The interior was simple, with only the airframe and the outside aluminum-skin between passengers and the elements. Along each side ran an aluminum bench for seating, with room on each side for eight or ten persons. There were only half-a-dozen people on board the flight.

The pilot was a Marine sergeant, as was the copilot. The officer member of the crew was the official courier responsible for safe handling of communications between Guadalcanal and New Caledonia. No planes were in line at the runway. We simply entered from the taxi strip, revved the engines, gathered speed going down the runway, and took off. Turning sideways, I could look out and down through a small side-window, and obtain a fairly good look at the island as we departed. There was a lot of ocean water between Guadalcanal and New Caledonia. The weather was good, and the flight entirely uneventful. It took probably four or five hours to cover the distance.

Arriving at New Caledonia, we entered the landing pattern at Tontouta Airfield, took our place in the circling-pattern of incoming planes, and made our landing. We then taxied down the runway and stopped just short of the control tower. "This is it, folks," the crew chief told us. "We have to refuel, reload, and return. You lucky people are now on your own."

# Impressions of
# Tontouta Airfield & Noumea

Things were really informal at Tontouta. No administrative office or tent, no check-in place, no vehicle and driver waiting for arrivals, no nothing. The crew chief obviously knew what he was talking about: each of us was now strictly on our own. A Navy chief saw me looking around and came over. "Where are you headed for?" he asked. "Camp Barnes," I replied. "That's in town," he said. "It's a nice location along the beach. I can give you a ride into town if you like."

During the drive, I learned from the chief that Tontouta Airfield was probably fifteen miles north of Noumea, the capital city and port facility. Noumea was also the Headquarters of the United States Armed Forces in the South Pacific Area (USAFISPA for short); and the location was known as "Camp Barnes." Nearby was a tent city, an Army field hospital and – also nearby, in more permanent structures – a Navy hospital. The island was a French colony now being governed by Free French. Its importance to France was the large deposits of nickel ore which were mined by the native population under supervision of French mining engineers. The ore was high-grade, and much needed in the war effort. It also provided large revenues for France.

The chief went out of his way to get me as far as downtown Noumea, and dropped me off in front of an obviously deserted hotel. "This is as far as I can get you in your direction," he told me, "but you can safely stay at this place. It's in the process of being taken over by the Navy for conversion into a rest and recuperation facility. It has no management yet, but is being used for transients like yourself. In the morning, you can stop any Army vehicle which you see in town. All of them will be going out to Camp Barnes. Good luck!" He waved and was off.

138

Going inside, I found Navy cots set up, each with a rolled-up mattress; no bedding or blankets of any kind, and not a single person in evidence. It was after working-hours and all had apparently departed. A couple of bunks had the mattress laid down and personal gear spread on top. Having no personal gear, I went out onto the street for a look around. The streets were bare of people. There were a few department stores, one still open. The window had no displays of any kind – and inside, the counters were nearly bare of goods. A few French-speaking clerks were still on duty, and I learned my first bit of French in response to my greeting: The standard reply was simply "ne comprends!" – which worked equally well for myself. I checked the neighborhood and, finding no eating establishments of any kind, worked my way back to the hotel which did have a name: "Hotel du Commerce." Inside, I found a washroom and toilet facility still in operation. This I made use of, returned to my bunk room, rolled out a mattress, and slept until daybreak.

## Reporting for Duty at Camp Barnes

By this time, I was fairly hungry, as you can well imagine – so I made my way to the street and flagged down the first Army truck which came into view. The driver stopped, and in response to my "How about taking me to Camp Barnes?" simply replied, "Sure, hop in." Five miles or so along the sandy beach of a natural harbor, we came to what was obviously Camp Barnes. The driver dropped me off at the gate, and with a wave and a "good luck" – was on his way again.

Approaching the sentry at the main gate, I stated my business and asked directions. I looked about as I waited. The office section of the camp was made up of plywood-construction engineering shacks, while the living section consisted of six-man tents, set on top of wooden platforms raised about a foot above ground-level. The street was dirt, and at the moment:

139

very dusty dirt. The main administrative shack was easy to find when pointed out by the sentry. It was the one with a flag flying directly in front.

The walk was short. I made my way to the flagpole, and saw that the shack in question had an open door. I approached, gave a knock on the doorpost, and entered.

Inside, behind a portable field-desk, sat a corporal, obviously the duty clerk at this early hour. "Good morning," I spoke. "I'm Larry Drew reporting from the 25th Division on Guadalcanal, and…" He interrupted: "Good morning to you. We knew that you were coming, but weren't sure of the date or time. You look hungry," he said as he focused on my face. "Let me point out the mess hall and you can get a breakfast right now. Then," he added, "just come back here. I'll get you settled and an issue of gear. You can leave your personnel file and shaving gear here." Handing over my Army personnel-file and shaving gear, I left and made my way to the camp mess hall, which obviously operated around-the-clock to suit the needs of the men who worked at different duty-shifts.

The mess hall was clean, and large enough to seat two- or three hundred men at a single sitting. It was nearly empty except for the food counter, which was well-laid-out and ready for business. No need to show orders or identify yourself – just pick up a tray, plate, cup, eating utensils, and become the first in line. I don't remember what I had for breakfast; it was a typical Army breakfast, well-prepared and all the seconds you wanted. I'm sure that I had pancakes – I always did if they were available. This fondness for pancakes became a lifelong habit of mine. I would do the research on where the best were, whose were just average, and – who you would "never-hit-again" for seconds!

I'm sure that the Camp Barnes mess also had eggs, sausage, and coffee. This was enough for me, since one could have seconds. It wasn't too long before I had successfully erased the hungry-look so easily recognized by the duty corporal at headquarters. I thanked the cooks and departed, making my way back to the headquarters shack and the duty corporal.

"You look a lot more human than you did when you checked in," he greeted me. "First, I'll show you to your assigned tent, because supply hasn't opened yet; then we'll go to supply, and then to your temporary duty assignment. Oh, yes," he went on, "I see you're here for the West Point Board, but it doesn't meet for three days. In the meantime, your talents are going to be used by USAFISPA. That's the way it is here, because we're short-handed in the technical areas."

We walked together down and across rows of six-man tents, all of which looked exactly the same as all the others. We finally stopped at one. "This is your assigned billet," the corporal said. "Inside, you will find a canvas Army cot made up and ready for you. All you have to do is memorize the location so that you can find it again. I do it by counting," he added. "So many rows back from the road, and so many tents down from the corner. It works for me. See, I'll do it with you…" Together we counted – and I memorized.

Back at the dirt road once more, we turned and made our way to what was obviously the supply shack. I recognized it by the vehicles around it and the stacks of material and provisions inside a secured, fenced compound. The corporal and I entered. He introduced me to the duty clerk and indicated that I was to receive a standard issue of clothing and gear: everything from socks, underwear, shirts, slacks, overseas caps, handkerchiefs, towels, soap, shoes, belts, and raincoat. "No steel helmets, rifles, ammunition, canteens, or aid kits here," he said. "This is Army Headquarters and we're a thousand miles from the fighting. Leave your issue here for now. I'll take you over to Headquarters Map Section and introduce you. Then you can come back here to get your gear and take it to your tent. I'll show you the toilet and shower facilities on the way. After you're all done with that, you're to return to the map section. You belong to them for the rest of the day – and succeeding days…" he added, "until one of us finds you in time to report to the examining board."

# Map Drafting and Intelligence Section

Back along the dirt road, not far from the headquarters shack, we came to another engineering-shack (which looked exactly like all the others), and entered. There were two men at work inside; both looked up as we entered, and both greeted the corporal. "Here's your new temporary man, Dick," he greeted the staff sergeant. "This is Corporal Larry Drew, fresh back from Guadalcanal." To me, he spoke: "And this is Sergeant Dick LaCoussier, who is in charge of the Map Drafting and Intelligence Section. This is the rest of the section: Corporal Ed Morrisette." We all shook hands and exchanged greetings. "Drew," the corporal said, "still has some personal things to do – like taking a shower and getting into a change of clothes. Then he will be back, and will belong to you for as much as he is allowed. He will, as you know, be pulled off now-and-then for other business; but in general, is available to you."

The front room of the map section was stacked high with map cases containing drawers about 4 inches high, 4 feet wide and 3-1/2 feet deep. The room contained only map cases and a single drafting table with a sign: "Sergeant LaCoussier." An identical room to the rear contained more map cases and four drafting tables. LaCoussier spoke, "Ed is sure glad to see you! He has been eating four meals a day and is lucky if he gets six hours of sleep at night. This has been going on for so long that he thinks it is normal…and," he laughed, "all for corporal's pay. You may just as well be warned now, because that is what is in store for you too. Your first job has already been lined-out and assigned. You, my good man, are going to produce the invasion maps for the New Georgia Campaign. That's appropriate after all, because your division will be leading the invasion."

142

Leaving the map section, I returned to my tent for soap, shaving kit, and towel – and then on to the shower and toilet facility. It was a really good facility, and large enough that people would not have to stand in line. It was the first fresh and hot water shower that I had had since leaving Schofield more than eight months earlier. How I enjoyed it! Equally, I enjoyed the hot-water shave which did not involve the use of my steel helmet. Refreshed, I got into a fresh change of clothes, dropped my gear off at my tent, and made my way back to the map section.

Once again, I received a warm welcome from LaCoussier and Morrisette, and was then shown to my drafting table in the rear office where Morrisette worked also. LaCoussier showed me the drafting supplies and the meager charts and maps which he had: mostly very small-scale, "National Geographic" prints, and the common atlas. For the next day or so, I would help Morrisette with his work to enable me to get the feel of what they were doing.

Midmorning, two other men drifted in and were introduced to me: Staff Sergeant Howard Brodie and Sergeant Mac Morris. Both were loosely assigned as staff members of the Army Newspaper, *Yank* – copies of which I had seen occasionally. Brodie was in his late twenties, and had worked as a staff artist for the *San Francisco Chronicle* before his tour with the Army. Morris was the newspaper writer of the team. Both had been on Guadalcanal when I was there, although I hadn't heard of them before. We instantly shared the bond of Guadalcanal experiences. I could tell right away that both would be easy to like and get along with. They occupied the other two drafting tables in the back drafting room.

LaCoussier took his lead from officers in the Planning Section at USAFISPA. On need-to-know basis, he was advised in priority maps and charts to be originated, deadlines for completed work, and quantities required for distribution. Now and then, he would take a partially-completed work over to planning for review and critique. Ed or I would make any of the necessary changes – along with the continued work for completing the project.

# Meeting Tentmates:
# The Japanese Language Section of the Intelligence Unit

I was startled from sleep my first morning at Camp Barnes by the New Caledonia version of a Guadalcanal earthquake. This one was strong enough to jar a man from his bunk! Stirring, and with half-open eyes, I saw a mountain of muscle in the middle of the floor doing push-ups. Seeing me, the "mountain" stood, grinned, and extended a huge hand. "I'm Hamano," said he. "You must be Drew, our new tentmate. Welcome back from Guadalcanal! I do this every morning to keep in shape," he explained. "... Do two hundred of these and then go for a five-mile swim in the bay. It's nice out there early in the morning, and…I have the bay all to myself. I'm from L.A.," he added. "My family owned a bar over in Hollywood until internment; I was the bouncer for the establishment. You can understand why I'm such a fitness nut."

"There are five of us in this unit," Hamano continued. "We're the Japanese Language Section of the Intelligence Unit. The families of each of us are in internment now in Northern California at Tule Lake, north of Alturas. It's hard for us and them to understand why this was done, because we are just as loyal Americans as you are. The life there is hard, but they seem to be getting along OK. Well, enough of that…I've got to get my swim in. Welcome, and glad to have met you." With that, Hamano was gone. The others were still sleeping as I dressed,

144

ate, and set off to the map section for my first day at making maps.

While en route to the mapping shack from breakfast, a light bulb went on in my head. I had been wondering why I had been put in a tent with five Japanese, and Hamano had given me the answer: They, he had said, were the Language Section of Intelligence. I, I realized, was Mapping Section of Intelligence. The answer now was so obvious: tents were assigned on the basis of the unit you were working in. There were probably several in that row of tents occupied by only those persons in Intelligence. Satisfied, I continued on to the mapping shack and my awaiting drafting board.

# Helping Morrisette: New Georgia Maps

LaCoussier, Morrisette, and I visited a few minutes, and LaCoussier showed me his meager information on the New Georgia complex of islands in the Northern Solomons. The office atlas showed the islands as small dots in the ocean with names attached: New Georgia, Rendova, Kolombangara, and Ghizo. Ghizo, the smallest, was about seven miles long and three miles wide. My job was to create maps of each on reproducibles, where each island would be twelve to eighteen inches across – showing mountains, rivers, bays, swamps, etc. For information supporting this need, we sat down and immediately worked-up a request for aerial-photo coverage showing the most detail possible. While waiting for the photos, I helped Ed Morrisette with the lettering work on his most current project.

Figure 34. Map of New Georgia (US Army)
reprinted from *The 25th Division and World War 2*
(p 48), Cpt. Robert F. Karolevitz, ed., 1946,
Army and Navy Publishing Company.

# West Point Exam & Physical

That first week, day three on New Caledonia, I also met with the West Point Examining Board, and sat with the other six men who would be taking the written exam with me. Ray Stannard, the other man from the 25th Division, did not show up. No one knew where he was. I had not been feeling well those first days. I hurt and ached a lot and was really "off my feed."

The day after taking the written exam, the seven of us were taken over to the Army evacuation hospital for the physical exam portion of the exam. I passed the physical in good shape. The doctor in charge was the senior hospital physician and took quite an interest in us. While talking to me after the physical, he looked at me and asked how I was feeling. "Not too good recently," I answered; "…like the change in climate has caught up with me." "Which reminds me," the doctor said, "I forgot to take your temperature and health signs. Here…" He stuck a thermometer in my mouth. "We'll do this first."

A few moments later, he removed the thermometer, read it, and shook his head; got a second thermometer and tried again. Upon reading the second result, he felt my forehead and asked, "How long have you been off Atabrine?" "About a week," I answered. "I stopped when I left Guadalcanal." "So you should have," he replied. "And now I have the answer for why you're feeling "under the weather," as you say: you're coming down with malaria. We'll get you feeling better soon enough. Right now, it's off to the hospital with you." Taking up his pad, he wrote an order, picked up a field phone, and gave a quick command. The next thing I knew, I was being escorted to a bed in one of the hospital tent wards as a patient!

# One Really Sick Soldier

Those first days in the hospital, I was one really sick soldier. At first came the overall aching – like every part of my body had been well-hammered. My spleen up under the rib cage swelled; it was large and painful. When the contents of the swollen spleen went into the bloodstream, a high fever resulted. When this broke, chills set in – which were pretty much uncontrollable. All the while, I was being fed quinine: morning, noon, and night. In a matter of days, the spleen went down – the chills, ache, and fever stopped; and my appetite began to return. The West Point physician checked in with me every day and would stay for a visit each time – obviously proud of the men in his charge. I believe that I was the only one of the group hospitalized at that time. I learned that the Atabrine we had been taking was a suppressive, but as soon as we were taken off of it, the malaria germs already in our bodies would multiply: then came the malaria attacks.

# Meeting Fellow Patients

Beginning to feel better, I started taking notice of the other patients in my tent ward. A good half of them were black troops. Getting to know these men was an entirely new experience for me. I had never seen or known black persons before, even in college or at Pearl Harbor. These fellow soldiers were from all walks of life. Many had little or no education, coming from the Southern sharecropper's life. Many, too, were from factory cities such as Detroit and Cleveland. One of the men was obviously the most-educated person in our ward. Interestingly, the war had brought us together, and all patients – black and white – mingled well with each other. We exchanged thoughts and ideas, played poker together, and in general, all were good-humored and good-natured. A lot of kidding and banter went on, such as I had seen everywhere. These troops were anti-aircraft artillery men from Brigadier General Benjamin Davis' Artillery Brigade stationed between Noumea and Tontouta Airfield. They gained the reputation of a crack anti-aircraft outfit. They were proud of themselves and proud of their general: the first African American general for the United States Army.

I became good friends with one of the men I met in the hospital: Corporal Curtis Oswald Smith from Indiana. I don't recall what he was in hospital for, but we hit it off from first acquaintance and were soon close buddies. Smith went on to Infantry Officer Candidate School (Infantry OCS) in Georgia, and then into Army Counter-Intelligence Corps. I lost track of him after VJ Day.


# Signs of Health & A Ward in "Stitches"

Taylor, one of General Davis' artillery men, could even get a laugh from a situation no one else thought the least bit humorous. Sylvia, a first lieutenant and our day nurse, would arrive in the morning like a "breeze – with a ruler in hand." Her very first tour was down each aisle of sleeping patients, checking for a first-recognizable sign of returning health: a penile erection. Sighting such, she would give it a friendly whack with the side of her ruler, startling the person and erasing the result of his dream. It wouldn't be many days later that the man was seen fit to return to duty.

One morning, Taylor was ready: he grabbed his crotch as our nurse came by. In a voice that woke the sleepers he cried, "Oh lord, Miss Sylvia, not today. My man is still limping after what you did yesterday." Apparently, reducing a ward to laughter was the second sign of recovery, and Taylor was back to his unit the next day.

# The Hospital Ward – Layout & Routine

I was surprised at the size of a ward tent: probably twenty feet wide and forty feet long, allowing for a row of hospital beds on each side and a wide aisle down the middle. The day crew and the evening crew had a single nurse in charge with several "ward men" as assistants. The nurse parceled out medicine to each patient, saw that it was taken, and checked and recorded vital signs probably twice on each shift. The ward men did everything else: feeding those needing assistance, changing bed linen, providing and taking care of bed pans, wheeling patients to examination areas and treatment centers, bathing those who couldn't care for themselves. The ambulatory patients shifted for themselves.

# Regaining Strength

Just beyond the tent section was the beach and the bay. It was a wide, sandy beach sloping gently into the bay with a soft, sandy bottom allowing you to walk a half block into the water without reaching your shoulders. There were two sections to the beach: the officers' beach with a wire enclosure and a guard at either end, and the rest of the beach for the enlisted troops. The officers' beach was active almost exclusively in the evening and at night: couples sharing a blankct sprcad on the sand, barbecues, and other small groups. The enlisted beach was active mostly during the daytime.

When I began feeling stronger, a few of us scrounged some steel barrels and some planking. With these materials, we fashioned a float – complete with plank-top and a low diving board. Digging the sand from beneath the barrels, we obtained flotation, and moved it out some distance from shore to where the water was perhaps fifteen feet deep. There at high tide, a mooring line and anchor were attached, and the float left in place. There were only a few persons who used it, but it provided a lot of fun. I was a very poor swimmer; I would walk as far out as I could before surfacing and struggling out to the float. Once there, I would jump in and swim about, and then struggle back to shore. Most of the men were good swimmers. Yet, even though there were many times when I had the float and the beach all to myself, I never seemed to improve.

# Navy Perks

The Navy hospital, situated right next door to the Army evacuation hospital, was made of more permanent, plywood structures. The hospital compound even had a high, chain-link fence surrounding it, complete with guard personnel on the gate. The Navy operation was much more sophisticated than the Army. It was complete with large, walk-in refrigeration and freezer units, which meant things like milk, ice cream, and a much wider variety of foods for their personnel. They even had beer for the enlisted men! (This alone would allow for the guard at the gate!) I don't know what the allotment for each enlisted man was, but on many occasions I observed an enterprising sailor take a case of beer down to the beach and into the surf at low tide. There he would dig a hole and bury his beer far enough seaward that the lapping water would not uncover his cache. The idea was to use the cool, ocean water and wet sand to lower the temperature of his brew. Oftentimes after dark, I would hear the familiar sounds of an eager sailor splashing around out in the bay looking for his cache of submerged beer. Sometimes he found it, and sometimes he didn't.

# A Gift from the Red Cross

The Red Cross was in evidence in New Caledonia also. On one occasion, ladies of the Australian Red Cross came through the Army hospital and gave each of us a small sewing-kit with a durable, sheepskin leather cover. I treasured mine and used it quite often. It was the only free thing that I ever received from any Red Cross unit anywhere. American Red Cross women were seen in their uniform in the area, but those I saw were always in the company of an officer and, normally, as a passenger of a military vehicle. Officer personnel were of the U.S. Navy, U.S. Army, Free French Navy, Free French Army, New Zealand Air Force, and Australian Air Force. The American Red Cross ladies whom I saw seemed to have no preference as to branch of service or country of service represented.

# Healing & Reassignment:
# An Intentional Wound

There was a young chap in our tent being treated for a gunshot wound to his foot. In time, I became aware that the medical staff had decided that it was a self-inflicted injury. The damage was considerable because of the many small bones in the foot, but he was responding well to the surgical reconstruction. Upon healing, he was not discharged from service, but was assigned to a noncombat unit rather than being returned to any unit involved in combat-contact with the enemy. This, in my opinion, was to protect those who would be around him and dependent on his support – more than as a protection to himself. Those of us in the tent ward never had any negative thoughts or attitudes toward him, but the medical staff did; and I could see it in the way they dealt with him: as though he was a second-class serviceman.

# A Needless Death

Also in hospital, I met one of the Australian troops stationed on the island: Corporal Bruzz Cuthbertson from Perth, Australia. Bruzz was tall, fair, big, and good-humored. He was well-educated, and an actor by profession. He had studied and been involved in theater in England before the war and his being called into service. He was also known socially to the Australian Consul at Noumea.

One night, an American soldier was brought into the receiving tent. He was seriously ill. Instead of being taken care of properly, he was put to bed in the receiving tent, given a sedative, and left until the day shift arrived next morning. By the time the "day people" checked in on him, the man was dead.

Cuthbertson had the first bed in our ward, and was directly opposite the entry to the receiving tent. He had lain awake the previous night and observed all that had happened. Learning of the man's death, he had asked for explanation and had been told that it was none of his business.

Cuthbertson was not used to being replied to in such fashion and, when all inquiries went for naught, had gone directly to the Australian Consulate with his story. Next, Cuthbertson returned to the Army field hospital with the Consul and again asked for explanation. The U.S. Army retaliated, and Bruzz found himself in the Psycho Ward. I was allowed to enter the high-fenced enclosure to visit him, but he was isolated and forcibly detained. He was given sedatives, subjected to psychiatric interviews and counseling, and encouraged to reshape his recollection of what he thought he had observed. Bruzz was adamant. He damn well knew what he had seen. He was outraged that the hospital staff had needlessly caused the death of a serviceman, and wanted some corrective action.

The Australian Consul visited Bruzz regularly, but even he could not obtain Cuthbertson's release from the Psycho Ward. Finally, a compromise was agreed on: The U.S. Army would release Cuthbertson from the Psycho Ward, and the Australian Consul would see to it that Cuthbertson would be off the island and back to Australia the same day. No admission of any kind was made by the hospital.

# Working a Schedule around Malaria

As I felt stronger, I was allowed to return to Camp Barnes part-time during the day to work in the map section. I remained in the hospital at night, and was there for meals, medical checkups, and medication three times a day. When I improved sufficiently, I was released from the hospital, and allowed to return to Camp Barnes and full duty.

"Full-duty" work involved the usual sixteen-hour shifts at my drafting board: making detailed maps for the upcoming New Georgia Campaign. Eventually, however, I would begin to notice a familiar, painful swelling begin under my lower-left rib cage. Each day the swelling would increase, as did the overall aching. Finally chills, sweats, and fever would set in. Once again, I would be returned to the 27th Evacuation Hospital, located a short distance away along the beach. The first three or four days were the worst: with very-high fever, followed by bone-shaking chills and aching of the worst kind, which, in turn, were again followed by the recurring, very high fever. On those days, I was in a dazed state; I couldn't even remember eating. I'm certain that I was forced to take large amounts of water to avoid dehydration, but don't remember that either.

I don't recall how long I was in hospital at any one time – perhaps three weeks. Then, back to Camp Barnes for maybe a month – until another bout of malaria surfaced – and back to the

Army Evacuation Hospital for another three weeks; back to Camp Barnes again, etc. All told, I think that I was in hospital four times before leaving New Caledonia. I collected quinine as I could, and built up a modest personal-supply for emergency use should I have the need.

## An End to Sloppiness: Captain's Orders

The Commanding Officer of Headquarters Company, Headquarters USAFISPA, scheduled a mandatory, all-hands formation of the enlisted personnel in the company with all men in rank, immediately after reveille. When the first sergeant called the company to attention and turned the formation over to the captain, it was easy to see that the captain was not just a little agitated – he was really upset.

"Men," he said in his loudest voice. "Men, we are going to hold a reveille formation regularly from now on, until I tell you otherwise. I realize that most of you are specialist technicians, but that ranking does not bring with it a privilege of informality and sloppiness such as you customarily exhibit. From now on, and hear me well: You will fall in at reveille fully-dressed, in clean uniform, shaved and toileted, and ready to report to your workstation. This business of falling in casually, sloppily, and 'when, as, or if you choose' has come to a screeching halt. I hope I have made myself clear. First Sergeant," the Captain continued, "you may dismiss the company!"

There was immediate improvement in response to the Captain's order – quite probably, I thought, because the word was circulating that those who chose to remain unmilitary or patently-sloppy would find themselves being transferred as privates into the combat-infantry replacement pool in the Solomon Islands.

# Sergeant LaCoussier's French Connection

Sergeant LaCoussier came from the upper New England area and identified himself as French Canadian. He handled the French language quite as well as he did English, and had even been welcomed into the upper levels of the New Caledonia French Community headed by Madame Roland, wife of the Free French Consul, Monsieur Varin. Madame Roland had become the recognized and accepted "hostess" of Lt. General Harmon, Commanding General USAFISPA, who in his generosity had even made one of his "general's personal sedans" available – complete with Army driver – for Madame's use.

One evening, when LaCoussier had been invited to Madame's home for tea, he had insisted that I accompany him. I went and was cordially received by Madame, who then visited comfortably with LaCoussier. Both were speaking French, of course – taking time out now and then to exchange pleasantries with me in English.

Later, the attractive daughter arrived, and was introduced to me in English. She handled English well, with only a slight accent. Edit Roland was probably late teens: tall, slender, and quite pretty. She visited with me in my language while LaCoussier and Madame continued in French.

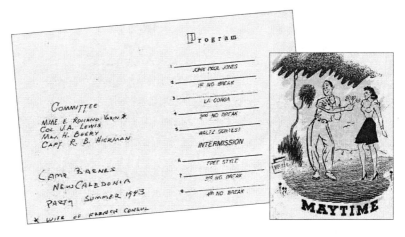

Figure 35.  Invitation from Headquarters Company USAFISPA to a
dance at Camp Barnes, 8 May 1943.  What a welcome change!

## Surprise Visits from a Pretty Friend

Thereafter, it seemed that I was Edit's friend. She would come
to visit at the drafting-hut unannounced, and also visit when I
was in hospital. Edit was driven on these visits by an Army
driver in what was obviously a sedan of General Harmon's. The
occasions were funny, if only because of the reactions of the
Army doctors and nurses at the arrival of the general's sedan. It
would be left parked in a "no-load zone," with the Army driver
still at the wheel, and Edit inside the ward-tent delivering aid
and comfort to the delighted, sick and wounded occupants of
the ward. Although Edit came to see me, she was quite friendly
to each of my colleagues; and they thought she was great.

On one of her unannounced visits, a Camp Barnes friend, Bill Bailey, was visiting also. Bill was a Southern lad, not much older than Edit. He was tall and well-built, with black hair that fairly glistened, a wide, warm smile, and "handsome-as-all-get-out." When Edit arrived, Bill – to use an expression deficient in originality – "only had eyes for her!" I introduced them, and when she was ready to depart, Edit offered to drop Bill off at Camp Barnes. After that day, her visits to the map section or hospital to see me became noticeably less and less. She continued to remain warm and friendly, but now it was Bill who was a much more important part of her life.

# A Promotion & New Duty Assignment

Perhaps a month after arriving at Camp Barnes, I received orders promoting me from corporal to sergeant. Ed Morrisette was on the same orders and became Sergeant also. A short while later, I received a letter from my buddy, Lenzie Russell, still with the battery and still on Guadalcanal. In his letter, he first congratulated me on being promoted to Sergeant; then he thanked me for his being promoted to Corporal. My being promoted had released the former Corporal's position and, this time, Gordon got his wish. After all, Lenzie Russell was "his man!"

Of the seven of us who had appeared before the West Point Examining Board, no one would make it to West Point. Accordingly, each of us was scheduled before the Officer Candidate Board. I don't know where the others were selected to go, but two of us were to be sent to the Field Artillery School at Fort Sill, Oklahoma. The orders were cut on 13 June 1943, to the effect that I was to proceed by "first available water transportation," returning to the continental U.S. and on to Fort Sill, Oklahoma where I had been scheduled to attend Officer Candidate School (OCS) Class "91."

# Some Stateside Requests

The Japanese-Americans I shared my tent with were delighted when they heard that I would be returning Stateside. Each had a personal request for me. Hamano had a beautiful and expensive watch. "Would you send it on to my father when you reach San Francisco?" Joe Yoshiwara's family, including his kid sister, were interned at Tule Lake. "Would you please purchase the things they need, package them, and mail them off to Tule Lake?"

I don't recall what the others asked, but I did as each requested. When my mother heard about Joe's family, she contacted them and continued to send needed items. My tentmates were all good guys, and each had accepted and treated me well. Serving their country in uniform, they would remain in the Pacific until after war's end.

# Chapter 8.
# Homeward Bound

## Returning Stateside

I am uncertain as to when I left New Caledonia. After saying my goodbyes to new friends around Camp Barnes, I was driven into Noumea and down to dockside. There, I was processed on board a Dutch ship waiting pierside, taking on a large cargo of nickel ore to ballast the otherwise empty ship. She was a World War I sister of the World War II ship, *Noordam*, which had taken us to Guadalcanal. This older ship was a *straight-diesel* engine-driven vessel; the newer ship, being a *diesel-electric* driven ship, was much quieter and faster. They were owned by the "Holland America Line" steamship company, and under contract to the U.S. Government.

There were possibly twenty Army enlisted men and no officer personnel on the return voyage. The ship travelled with no escort. The trip was quiet, as the Pacific Ocean was relatively calm, and we were too insignificant to interest an enemy ship. There was no duty for anyone to serve during the trip. We had the run of the ship, lots of room for walking and exercising, and the food was good and plentiful. I have no recollection whatever of the ship's crew, or even if the ship had a Navy armed guard or not – but I think not. On heading home, we crossed the equator with no fanfare whatever; after all, we had obviously crossed it before, and were recognized as shellbacks. The days went by, and soon we would be seeing the coast I had left so many months before.

# San Francisco Bay

Late morning of August 2nd, I could see that our ship was approaching shore. A coastal range of mountains was growing visible. Then, low on the horizon, I could make out what was obviously the span of a large bridge – which continued to grow ever larger and higher. I knew it had to be the Golden Gate. How long ago – and how many miles past – had it been since last seen on the outbound trip which had taken me to Pearl Harbor and then on to Guadalcanal!

Past Alcatraz Prison Island, proceeding under the Bay Bridge, and further into San Francisco Bay, we finally sighted piers for ocean-going vessels. Singling out one in particular, we approached, and tied up. Our ship had arrived!

Shortly after docking, our group of enlisted men were approached by an Army enlisted man, obviously in authority. We were told to assemble. It was clear that we were about to go ashore. But then the question arose: "Were we?!" While standing with my gear, midship on the main deck, I grew uneasy.

# Angel Island:
# An Unexpected Diversion

Taking my gear, I made my way down the ship's gangplank, then, following instructions, made my way across the pier and – again, following instructions: up another gangplank and onto another, smaller vessel. No sooner had the group of us boarded than the gangplank was raised, and the ship cast off. Off we set back into the bay once more. We were treated to a return view of Alcatraz. It came closer and closer – then we passed it and continued on further into the bay, where our guide found another island.

"This..." our guide told us, "this is Fort McDowell, which is located on Angel Island. It is the Army Port of Embarkation for overseas, and the port of debarkation for personnel returning from overseas."

Our vessel reached a pier, pulled alongside, docked, and was tied up. "Pick up your gear, men," our guide told us. "Pick up your gear and follow me to your new 'temporary home.'"

There was only one serviceable pier at Fort McDowell. Along the waterfront and perhaps a city-block inland, were buildings consisting of two-story, frame structures: Headquarters building; half-a-dozen barracks; a small, Post Exchange; a laundry; and a mess hall. The rest of the garrison's structures had been torn down with only bare, concrete slabs giving evidence of former glory. The Stars and Stripes flew from a pole in front of the Headquarters building.

There was a single, high hill in the center of the island, some trees and shrubs, and a dirt road that indicated one could follow it and walk around the island. Angel Island might have been a mile or so across. The present population was obviously small. It was at least twice as far from San Francisco as Alcatraz.

It was only a short walk from the pier to the barracks assigned us. Inside, the barracks were clean and tidy, with bunks already set up, made up, and awaiting our arrival. Our "corporal guide" told us that we could select whatever bunk we wished, grab a shower, and that he would return in half an hour to take us to the mess hall. The shower was great: fresh water, hot water, and all you wanted; no water restriction.

The enlisted mess hall was large and well-furnished – obviously ready for much larger groups than ourselves. The meal was outstanding for the Army: almost as good as I had come to take for granted from Sergeant McKee. We had steak, vegetables, salad, coffee, milk, water with ice floating in it, different choices of cake and pie, ice cream, and seconds – all one wanted!

## "Under Quarantine for the Present"

After lunch we were visited by an officer assigned to duty at the fort. He announced to us that the Army had been instructed by the U.S. Government to prevent, in so far as possible, the introduction of diseases and infections unknown in the continental U.S.A. He then went on to explain: "You are," he said, "under quarantine for the present." "For how long?" He had "no idea!" We would be expected to pull small details of duty while there, and would be subject to physical inspections. These would include a regular physical exam, with unannounced spot-check exams during the day – and also at any hour of the night!

That first afternoon on Angel Island, an Army doctor and two-or-three Medical Corps enlisted assistants had us assemble in our barrack, where each of us was given a comprehensive medical exam and inspection. This included a rectal and prostate exam, and the customary "short-arm" inspection of the "private parts," checking for venereal disease. Blood samples were taken for laboratory examination, and skin-scrapings for bacteriological culture evaluations.

# A Lousy Home-Coming

The rest of that first evening was ours to use as we wished. For the most part, we spent our time at the waterfront watching the skyline across the bay to the south. It was completely filled with the twinkling lights of San Francisco. How strange, I thought – after being away so very long – to observe the city in such a cold, unreachable manner! None of us had ever been in an isolation quarantine before, and to say the least, the message received was that we were unwelcome – and even resented. When we had landed, there was not a single sign or word of greeting, or "Welcome Back!" Rather, it seemed our arrival was seen as just another duty or problem for someone to handle!

True as been told, the first night we were wakened about midnight and also two-or-three hours later by Army medics. All of us were turned out and inspected. The indignity was strongly and vocally resented.

That next morning after breakfast, we were assembled and divided into small work-parties. No one was assigned to the kitchen: after all, we might introduce a new disease or ailment. The jobs involved cleaning toilet facilities in the officer barracks; stripping beds in the officer quarters and remaking them with fresh linens; sweeping the officer barracks; grounds cleaning and litter pickup. They even had us cleaning the officers' shoes!

Each of the twenty of us were sergeants, each had been overseas and involved in ground or aerial combat, to the extent that we had been selected to attend OCS and to share what we had learned with Stateside troops. Now, we were being assigned to orderly duty for a bunch of young, new, inexperienced officers on their way overseas to replacement pools! Was there some reason they couldn't care for themselves? They had better be able to do so!

Again, the medical personnel showed up to give us examinations; afterwards, we had the rest of the afternoon and evening free. Some of the men wrote letters, others became involved in card games. Unable to work up much enthusiasm from the others for a hike, I spent the afternoon exploring the shoreline on my own.

That evening, we clustered together in small groups at water's edge and gazed at the lights of San Francisco far across the bay! At night, we were again awakened for the medical inspections – always at odd hours. The resentment we were feeling was well-vocalized, yet always went unanswered by the medics.

On 2 August, I sent a telegram to my family in Westboro advising that I had arrived in the USA.

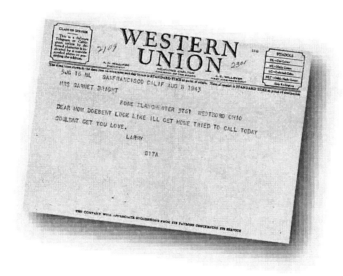

Figures 36-39. A series of telegrams to and from my mom
as to when I might be able to get home to Ohio.

On 8 August, after an unsuccessful attempt to phone home, I sent a second telegram.

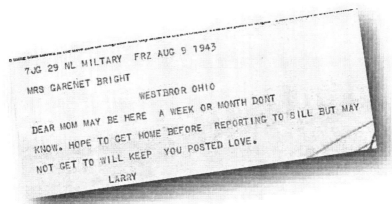

DEAR MOM MAY BE HERE A WEEK OR MONTH DONT KNOW. HOPE TO GET HOME BEFORE REPORTING TO SILL BUT MAY NOT GET TO WILL KEEP YOU POSTED LOVE.
LARRY

I didn't know how long I would be detained at Fort McDowell and had orders to report at Fort Sill by 19 August. So on 9 August, I sent a third telegram wiring my uncertain status to those at home: "…so, maybe I will be able to get back to Westboro and maybe not."

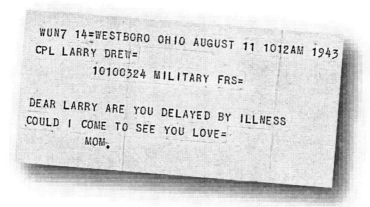

DEAR LARRY ARE YOU DELAYED BY ILLNESS COULD I COME TO SEE YOU LOVE=
MOM.

During free-time, I made use of the well-stocked Post Exchange and took many hikes, exploring the shoreline and central hill areas of the island. Across the bay to the north were also hills, largely covered with pine forests and a very few homes. It all looked beautiful and inviting, yet remained off-limits.

In stark contrast to our situation, officer personnel awaiting transportation overseas had no duty of any kind, and were allowed to go ashore from morning until the last-returning boat at night. They did, however, elect to make their own bunks after the first day of our service. When we made up their bunks, we had put the bottom sheet down full-length, and overlayed it with the top sheet, folded in half and tucked tightly in ("short-sheet" in Army talk). With this arrangement, when the occupant tumbled into bed and attempted to stretch out, he found his feet blocked midway by the short sheet. The then-grumpy lieutenant had two choices: he could stretch out full length on top of the sheet, or he could tear his bunk apart and do it properly himself. Next morning, the noncom in charge of "officer bed-making" complained to us about the short-sheeting. He received a bland reply. We had no idea how or why it had happened, but we would not be the least surprised if it were to continue unabated.

About 10 August, we were told to turn in all of our summer uniforms and draw Army wool uniforms! In August? "Well," came the reply, "the wool uniform is the only official Army uniform, and you are to wear it at all times when on leave or in travel status." We all changed to hot, olive-drab wool, and each went through the Post Taylor Shop for the addition of sergeant stripes and overseas hash marks.

Still, part of each afternoon and two-or-three times each night were spent on "short arm" and personal-health inspections. By now, it was recognized as a necessary evil; and we and the medics had adopted an attitude of general, good-natured banter on the indignity. "Just wait until you return from overseas and see how you feel about receiving what you're giving out!" "What makes you think we'll be getting inspected?" they replied. "After all: We're the Medical Corps!"

My last day at McDowell was 12 August. I was in the Exchange having a beer when who should walk in – but

Gordon! We spotted each other instantly, and he joined me as soon as he got himself a beer.

"Damn, Gordon!" were my first words. "Damn, I had been told that you were dead!" "Well, it's really me! It's been such a long time that I've been gone, and now I'm really back...I'm sure glad to be back!" – came all at once. Gordon, it turned out, was on his way to Fort Sill, as was I. He would be in an Officer class four-or-five weeks after mine began. We talked well into the night, cementing a friendship that lasted well into our old age. The next day, the Army ferry took our group of twenty off the island to begin our separate ways.

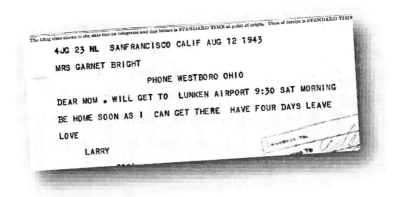

The filing time shown in the date line on telegrams and day letters is STANDARD TIME at point of origin. Time of receipt is STANDARD TIME

4JG 23 NL   SANFRANCISCO CALIF AUG 12 1943

MRS GARNET BRIGHT

PHONE WESTBORO OHIO

DEAR MOM . WILL GET TO  LUNKEN AIRPORT 9:30 SAT MORNING

BE HOME SOON AS I  CAN GET THERE  HAVE FOUR DAYS LEAVE

LOVE

LARRY

Figure 39.  Telegram to Mom. Good news, at last!

# Homeward Bound - Finally!

My orders stated a "Priority #4" for air transportation through 20 August 1943, and a "Priority #1" rail authority through the same date. At the Army pier, several of us boarded the waiting Army truck which took us directly to San Francisco Airport. There, I had no difficulty obtaining an air ticket from San Francisco to Cincinnati.

I arrived in Cincinnati, Ohio on 13 August, and was allowed a "four days and three nights" leave before leaving by train from Cincinnati to Fort Sill, Oklahoma.

Four days at home were probably enough for a returning serviceman. Practically all of the young men whom I had known in high school were in service and gone. The few who may have been "dodging the draft" didn't particularly wish to be seen by those of us who were returning. I visited Pop and Grandma, and enjoyed dinner with them – then later visited Rusty Nicely's mom and dad. Rusty was in Iceland with the Army. Walter Van Pelt, who lived on the farm next to Grandma's, saw me walking in, dropped his work, and ran to see and welcome me. It was very touching. Walter had to live with the threat of seizures. He never knew when he might have one, or what might set it off. Thus, his welcome was doubly touching.

## Invitation to a Home-Coming Party

Mom and Virgil Bright were married and keeping house at Virgil's farm. Virgil had planned work to share with me when I arrived – things that were too heavy for one person to do. I remember working a day or two of my furlough with him. He seemed to appreciate it. Mom told me that she had baked my favorite cake in honor of my coming home. To save my soul, I couldn't remember what my favorite cake was supposed to be. That evening, I learned it was chocolate with chocolate icing!

Invitation to a War

# Epilogue

Figure 40. A formal photograph of Larry taken in the
"…hot, olive-drab wool and 'only official' Army uniform…
(to be worn) at all times when on leave or in travel status!"

After his home leave, Larry went on to Officer Candidate
School (OCS) at Ft. Sill, Oklahoma, where he earned his
lieutenant bars. He then led a training platoon at Ft. Bragg,
North Carolina, where he was recruited for "hazardous overseas
duty," by the Office of Strategic Services (OSS). Specialized
training and a long sea voyage found him in India preparing to
drive the Burma Road into China. His assignment was to train
and lead Chinese soldiers into battle against Japanese forces.
These adventures are the subject of another book to follow.